THE
PHANTOM
PRINCE

MY LIFE
WITH
TED BUNDY

UPDATED AND EXPANDED EDITION

THE
PHANTOM
PRINCE

MY LIFE
WITH
TED BUNDY

UPDATED AND EXPANDED EDITION

ELIZABETH KENDALL
WITH A CONTRIBUTION FROM MOLLY KENDALL

ABRAMS PRESS, NEW YORK

Library of Congress Control Number: 2019951722

ISBN: 978-1-4197-4485-3
eISBN: 978-1-68335-952-4

Printed and bound in the U.S.A.
10 9 8 7 6 5 4 3 2 1

The material contained in this book is presented only for informational and artistic
purposes. In the interest of maintaining the privacy of the individuals whose stories are
discussed herein, many names, places, and other identifying characteristics have been
changed.

ABRAMS The Art of Books
195 Broadway, New York, NY 10007
abramsbooks.com

Molly and I know that we are incredibly fortunate to have each other. As we set about to tell our stories, we begin at a place of remembrance of those who were killed and compassion for the survivors, and for the families of all of Ted's victims. —EK

— CONTENTS —

— INTRODUCTION TO THE UPDATED EDITION —

In May 2017, I learned via the Internet that a new Ted Bundy movie was being made, and the story was going to be told from the perspective of Bundy's longtime girlfriend. I did a quick Internet search and got twenty-one thousand hits—all announcing the news about "my story" being told in a new Ted Bundy movie. I was stunned. How could they tell my story without ever speaking with me?

It had been a long time since Ted Bundy's terrible crimes had saturated the media. I had hoped it would stay that way. Sure, his name had become shorthand in popular culture for a person who looks normal but is in fact dangerous. However, aside from the past's occasional intrusion into the present, I had mostly been able to go about my life without Ted Bundy interfering with my happiness. Now that was all about to change.

Most books and movies had used either a made-up name for me or the pseudonym I used for my book, but a press release for the movie had used my real name. At least what my name had been. I haven't gone by my old married name of Kloepfer for years, not since Molly was a child. Unfortunately, some still link the name to Ted Bundy.

I began getting inquiries from documentary filmmakers and media outlets, which I referred to my attorney. They assumed that since I had optioned my book to the movie studio, I would be willing to speak with them now. Of course, there had been no book option. Molly and I turned all this over to the attorneys to sort out.

In the meantime, we had many conversations about how to deal with the renewed interest in this part of our lives. On the one hand, we would have been happy if interest in Ted Bundy and his sickness faded away into the nothingness that it deserved. On the other hand, if the story was going to be told again, the only way we could influence the outcome was to work with the film and documentary makers. We decided this was the most empowering way to proceed.

After getting off on the wrong foot initially, the collaboration we had with the film was a good one. We were happy to find that director Joe Berlinger respected and acted upon our input. Everyone associated with the production was kind and treated us well.

We were able to face our fears and watch the finished film. It was well-directed and well-acted. We were left with the feeling that Zac Efron and Lily Collins got it right.

Even so, during the filmmaking process, we realized that with the dramatization of a true story, things must be omitted, condensed, or combined to help the story fit within time constraints. Molly and I decided that it was essential that we tell our story in our own words as we experienced it, which was why we decided to issue this second edition of *The Phantom Prince*.

This is also what motivated me, after so many years of silence, to participate in the Amazon Original documentary series *Ted Bundy: Falling for a Killer* from director Trish Wood. I was interested in this project because of its emphasis on the viewpoints of many of the women involved in this tragic story. Trish and her crew from Saloon Media in Ontario, Canada, made the trek to Seattle several times with all their gear—cameras, sound equipment, lights, etc.— for interviews. They provided a calm and safe environment to talk about a difficult subject. For these projects, I have used my original pseudonym, Elizabeth Kendall, to spare Molly's father's family name further association with Ted's crimes.

In addition to the original text, you will find many photos of Ted and us from the years of my relationship with him, before the cloud of suspicion appeared on the horizon, as well as photos taken after the point when we now know Ted was abducting and killing young women.

I have written an afterword that follows the original text. I still cared deeply for Ted when I wrote the original book. It took years of work for me to accept who he was and what he had done. I still felt lingering shame that I had loved Ted Bundy. It was healing for me when women started telling their stories of sexual violence and assault as part of the Me Too movement. I could relate to keeping experiences secret for fear of being judged. I could see these women were taking back their power by saying, "This is what happened. It is what it is." This is true, too, of my past with Ted Bundy.

To close the book, Molly has written an account of her experiences with Ted. This is the first time she has told her story publicly.

Healing and rebuilding our lives after the trauma of knowing how evil and immoral Ted Bundy was has been anything but linear. Often it felt like two steps forward and one step back. Sometimes Molly and I were in sync with our thoughts and feelings about the past, and sometimes we were not. Even so, we knew our love for each other would help us heal, move forward, and never give up.

In writing this book, I have gone through a wide range of feelings towards Ted. At times, the intensity of my love for him scared me. When I thought of some of the happy times we shared, I was overwhelmed by the feeling that he should not be in jail. But by the time I finished my writing, those feelings had turned to outrage that he had coldly, capriciously murdered all those women. It has been seven years since that first cloud of worry passed through my mind and it has been three years since I have known that my fears were true, yet some days it hits me as if for the first time.

In 1974, when the victims were disappearing, I identified with them even though I was older than they were, and I feared for my own safety. Seven years later as I wrote my story, I identified them with my daughter and could imagine the pain Ted Bundy caused their parents and the terrible void left by their deaths.

In spite of all the destruction he has caused around him, I still care what happens to Ted. I have come to accept that a part of me will always love a part of him. He is no longer a part of my day to day life, though. Writing this book has been like having a tumor removed from my brain.

Naively, I thought I would carry the secret of my involvement in Ted's arrest to the grave, but it wasn't long after his conviction that reporters, writers, and private investigators began showing up at my office and home, all with their own reason why I should tell them what really happened. I declined. I knew my decisions and motivations would never be understandable unless I told my own story from beginning to end. I thank Dan Levant for giving me that opportunity. I would also like to thank Ann Adams and my attorney, Glenna Hall, for their help. A special thanks to my boss for the moral support he gave me throughout those hard years and for his continued support while I was writing this book.

One of the people who read the book in manuscript said something that disturbed me: "You're asking people to feel sorry for you. My God, people died! You're one of the lucky ones—you lived!" I want to answer that. Never did I forget that real women had been murdered for no other reason than they were attractive and friendly. The hideous reality of their deaths became my reality, too. Their tragedy was my trauma. For a long time, I lived with the guilt of wondering if Ted saw me in these women, if killing them was a sick, compulsive effort to kill something he hated in me. I am thankful to have survived, thankful for the chance to work my problems through, thankful for the resiliency God gives humans.

I am also thankful for my parents and my family who love me no matter what, for my eighty-four-year-old aunt who teaches me how to live and love by her example, for my friends who are always there when I need them (and I need them lots), for Hank who helped me break away from a destructive relationship, for Angie who helps me grow spiritually, for my recovery sponsor who made me learn about myself, but most of all for my daughter, who is a very, very special young woman.

— CHAPTER ONE —

Monday, March 1, 1976. I sat in a cold courtroom in Salt Lake City next to Ted Bundy's parents. It was snowing outside. Ted sat at the defense table with his attorneys, waiting for the judge to return with the verdict. I stared at the back of Ted's head, my mind filled with memories of things we had gone through together for the past six years.

Ted Bundy was on trial for the attempted kidnapping of a young woman, Carol DaRonch, from a suburban shopping mall near Salt Lake City. She identified Ted as the man who, posing as a police officer, had lured her into his Volkswagen, handcuffed her, and tried to crush her head with a crowbar. Her attempted abduction had been linked to the disappearances and murders of several young women in the Salt Lake City area. And the Salt Lake murders were linked to eight murders of young women in the Seattle area during the first seven months of 1974.

Ted and I met in Seattle in October 1969, became lovers, and continued an intense relationship until September 1974, when he moved to Salt Lake City. Even now, a year and a half later, we were far from finished with each other. Since the summer of 1974, I had been tormented by fears that Ted was involved in the murders in the Seattle area. Finally, I had gone to the King County Police with my suspicions. They told me they had checked Ted out and eliminated him as a suspect. But I continued to worry, and in January 1975, I talked to the police in Salt Lake City. They also told me he was clear. Now I knew that I had been terribly mistaken, that my Ted could not be guilty of these horrible crimes, but that I had set in motion machinery of the law that could crush out his life.

Judge Stewart Hanson entered, and we all stood. There seemed to be no air in the room.

"I find the defendant, Theodore Robert Bundy, guilty of aggravated kidnapping, a first-degree felony."

Ted's attorney asked that Ted be allowed some time with his family. We entered the judge's chamber where Ted was frisked and his hands cuffed behind his back. I put my arms around him and told him I was sorry. He was drenched with sweat and stiff with tension. I kissed him on the cheek and whispered, "I love you." I hated myself for what I had done to him.

In July 1979, I watched Ted again as another verdict was read. This time the trial was in Florida and I was seeing it on TV. This time I was sure that Ted was guilty as charged: guilty of raping and beating to death two young women as they slept in their Florida State University sorority house and of severely beating three others. I knew he was guilty because of what he had told me in a 2:00 A.M. telephone call in February just after he was captured in Florida.

The Florida prosecutors had visited me in Seattle and asked me to testify against Ted. I had at first agreed, but the more I thought about it the more reluctant I became. I still cared about him very much, and I had worked very hard at putting my life back together. I was sure the defense could make mincemeat of my testimony and of me. I had never been named in the press, and I valued my anonymity. My sex life with Ted would be a subject of great interest, as it had been to all the investigating police officers. I was a recovering alcoholic—had not had a drink in three years—but people would only hear the word *alcoholic*.

The prosecutors had told me my testimony was vital and that they would protect me from attacks by Ted's lawyers, but I reminded them that in our 2:00 A.M. phone conversation, Ted had specifically refused to talk to me about the crimes in Florida. He was trying to arrange things so that he could be returned to a prison in Washington State and be near his family and friends. I asked the prosecutors why they didn't bargain with Ted, offer him this in exchange for answers to questions about the murders of young women in Washington, Oregon, Utah, and Colorado.

In a heavy southern drawl, one of them told me, "Mister Bundy is bargainin' for his life. We're bargainin' for his death."

I couldn't be a part of it. They saw Ted Bundy as a murderer. I knew him as a lover and a friend. I was threatened with extradition if I wouldn't cooperate, but finally the matter was dropped and I never heard from the Florida prosecutors again. It took the jury only six hours to come in with a verdict of guilty.

I can count on two fingers the times Ted threatened me or was the least bit violent towards me. Yet I feel that I have lived through a violent time. I have spent too much of the last six years thinking about beatings, strangulations, rapes, the outrage of the brutal deaths of innocent people, and my own guilt. The untrue things that have been written about me and my relationship with Ted are a different kind of outrage. This book is an attempt to rid myself of both nightmares by facing them down.

I left Utah in 1969, twenty-four years old and not pleased with the way my life was turning out. On the surface I was doing all right. I was in my last year of college at Utah State, getting grades good enough to make the dean's list. Not bad, considering that I'd been suspended for disciplinary reasons a few years earlier. My two-year-old daughter Molly was a great joy to me, and since she was the first grandchild on both sides of her family, I had help and support from all the grandparents.

On the other hand, my brief marriage to Molly's father had been a disaster. While I was relieved when our divorce was final, I was now acutely embarrassed about being a divorcee. I spent a lot of time trying to figure out what was wrong with me that I couldn't make my marriage work. I'd been given all the tools anyone needed to lead a successful life, but somehow, I had managed to screw up.

My dad was a respected doctor in Ogden, thirty miles north of Salt Lake City. My mom had been a nurse until my oldest brother was born, and then she became a dedicated stay-at-home mother. Our family wasn't active in the Church—we were considered "jack Mormons," people who were Mormons in name but didn't follow all the Church's rules. But I still knew that our ancestors had walked across America so that we could be Mormons. Mom and I prayed together when I was little, and I grew up knowing the power of prayer. I also knew that if you forgot to be grateful, God would get you.

By the time I got to high school all I wanted to do was spend time with my boyfriend, Ben. He had a black MGA sports car, and when we weren't out riding around in it, we were washing it, waxing it, and cleaning the wire wheels. We went skiing every chance we got, the ultimate in teenage chic as we tooled down the road in the shiny black MGA with the skis on the back.

Ben and I went steady all through high school. We were going to get married as soon as we graduated and have a baby and name him Stein after Stein Eriksen, a popular ski racer at the time. My parents had other ideas. They told me I needed a college education. I told them they would be wasting their money, because all I wanted out of life was to marry Ben and start having babies.

They won and I went off to college. I went through sorority rush and was dropped at the end of rush week. I hadn't really wanted to be a sorority girl, but I was surprised at how much it hurt. I figured it was my shyness that had done me in. When I was with my friends or with Ben, I talked constantly. I loved to laugh and make Ben and my friends laugh, but when I got around strangers, I could never think of anything to say, or I would say something really stupid and relive it for months. I turned red when I was spoken to, and the more I fought it, the redder I would get.

I began to party a lot, my grades crashed, and at the end of my freshman year, I was suspended. I also broke up with Ben, without being able to tell him why. Ben and I were strongly attracted to each other physically, but we had decided early in our relationship that we were not going to "go all the way" until we got married. In the spring of my freshman year I went to bed with a man for the first time—not Ben but Jim, the man I eventually married. When the marriage ended, I was on my own.

I had always been half of a couple—first Ben, then Jim. Now I was alone with a young daughter and a need to start over. Utah didn't seem like any place for a single parent, so I started thinking about moving. Angie, my friend since junior high school, had just had a bad experience as a VISTA volunteer, and she was looking for a fresh start, too. We considered San Francisco, where my sister lived, but decided it would be too sophisticated for us. At quarter break we went skiing at Sun Valley, met some guys there who were learning to set up a ski patrol for a new resort near Seattle, and were easily persuaded that Seattle might be the place. I even had a cousin living there, and I figured that having some family nearby would soften the lump-in-my-throat feeling I was having about leaving my family and familiar territory.

I had to stay around long enough to collect my degree, so Angie went on ahead by herself. I hung on in Utah until fall, when I decided it was now or never.

— CHAPTER TWO —

I fell in love with Seattle at first sight. My brother and his wife had pulled a U-Haul trailer with all my belongings behind their car, while Molly and I followed in my VW bug. We came into the city early one morning over one of the long floating bridges that cross Lake Washington. It had been raining, and mist was clinging to the tops of the evergreens. Everything that wasn't gray was green. There were sailboats on the lake, hills all around, and the University of Washington off to the right. I could hardly wait to get going on my new life.

Molly and I stayed with Angie and her two roommates in her Capitol Hill apartment until I found my own place. The city was a new world to me. There was water everywhere I looked: Lake Washington to the east, Puget Sound to the west, Lake Union in the middle, and a canal with locks that connected them all. Losing my sense of direction, I kept confusing one body of water with another. The street numbering was worse. There was one street called Fortieth N.E. and another called N.E. Fortieth.

Within a few days I found an apartment I could afford about twelve blocks from Angie's. I hadn't realized that rent would be a lot higher than in Utah and that I would have to pay the first and last months' rent in advance, along with a cleaning deposit. The place wasn't much—a one-bedroom, first-floor apartment in a 1950s building that looked like a motel. It was furnished with a turquoise naugahyde couch and matching chair, a Formica coffee table, and not much else. The kitchen was the size of a closet, and the refrigerator was the size of a TV set. On one side was a tiny lanai from which I could look up at the tall building next door. Molly, who had just turned three, would have to sleep on the couch until we could afford something better.

I looked for a job right away. My degree in Business and Family Life wasn't going to impress anybody, but I thought it could get me a good secretarial job. The University of Washington was my first choice—I was used to being a student—and I was encouraged when the University Personnel Department sent me out for an interview at the Medical School. As I walked out of the personnel office, ten or twelve police cars full of men in riot gear roared by. Trying to find my way across the campus a few minutes later, I came upon a huge construction site where a crowd was milling around with picket signs. Suddenly, a great howl went up from the crowd as some black men pushed a bulldozer off the edge of a hundred-foot-deep pit. As it crashed to the bottom, the riot police moved into the crowd. I stood clutching my map of the campus, lost. When I finally arrived for the interview, I was nearly forty-five minutes late.

The man who interviewed me (and later became my boss and my friend) told me not to worry about it—that the kind of thing I had just watched happened on Upper Campus, that down here in Health Sciences, things were a lot quieter. What I had seen was one of Seattle's most violent civil rights protests, an angry demand that more blacks be hired on the construction project. My interview went well and a few days later I was hired as a secretary in one of the university's medical departments.

Within a few weeks, my life in the city was taking shape. Not having grandmothers around to take care of Molly was a problem, but I was able to find a good daycare center in the University District. Some mornings Molly cried when I left her, and I didn't like the way I felt either. I thought it was important for mothers to mother their children and wondered how I could do a good job of mothering when I was at work eight hours a day. I called my parents a lot and wished

I could drop by for Sunday dinner, but all in all, I was pleased that I had started my new life.

Money. as always, was a worry. I counted my quarters and dimes carefully. One Saturday I put my clothes in a laundromat washer and Molly and I went across the street to visit with Angie. When I went back to put the clothes in the dryer, I found a parking ticket on my windshield. I leaned against the car and turned the ticket over to see how much the fine was. Twenty dollars!

I was sitting at Angie's kitchen table, still crying about the damn ticket, when one of her roommates' boyfriends came in. "What you need," he said, "is a night out. Let's find you a babysitter and go out and get rowdy." It didn't solve my money problem, but it sounded *good*. Angie's place was headquarters for a bunch of people we knew from Utah and their boyfriends and girlfriends. By nightfall, we had organized a party to celebrate my parking ticket.

When Angie and I got to the Sandpiper Tavern in the University District, our friends had started to gather. It was dark inside; people were dancing on an elevated dance floor to a jukebox stocked with Beatles and Jimi Hendrix hits, looking as if they had strolled out of their sorority or fraternity houses dressed in jeans and sweaters. It wasn't so different from Saturday night back home. After two beers, I decided that this was exactly what I needed. After a few more beers I didn't even feel shy.

The last bits of shyness disappeared when a tall, sandy-haired man invited me to dance. I had already sized him up from across the room. He looked a little older and better dressed than the rest of the crowd; I figured he must be a graduate student or maybe even an instructor.

"Do you come here often?" he asked as we danced.

"No," I said, "this is the first time I've been out since I moved to Seattle." He asked the inevitable "from where?" and I thought of saying San Francisco or some other place that sounded classy, but I admitted to Utah.

"Utah!" he exclaimed. "Isn't that in Wyoming?"

We laughed about where Utah really was—somewhere around the Great Salt Lake—and carried on as strangers in bars do, till the music stopped.

I danced with everyone who asked. Drinking and dancing go together, and every time I came back to the table the beer tasted better. I kept trying to catch the sandy-haired man's eye, but he was usually dancing with somebody else. We smiled at each other across the floor a couple of times, but he didn't ask me to dance again.

Later in the evening, a skinny young man asked me to dance and I did, even though Angie and I had just been joking about his taste in clothes. He turned out to be a creep, and looking for a chance to escape, I saw the sandy-haired man sitting by himself, looking sad. I headed for his table.

"You look like your best friend just died," I said. He looked up, surprised. "I said you look lower than a snake's belly in a wagon track."

"Is that how you folks from Utah talk?" he said. "What do you call yourselves? Utonians? Utahites?"

"Utaaaaahns," I told him in my best hick voice. He laughed and I sat down. He asked me if I was a student. I was tempted to say yes because I didn't like telling people I was a secretary. I told him I worked at the university, but then I found myself telling him that I made heart valves in the instrument department. I could feel my face turning red, so I started blabbing about living in Seattle for only a couple of weeks, about it raining all the time, about the riot I had seen on campus—anything to keep talking.

He wanted to know why I had moved away from Utah. I told him briefly that I had been married, that I had a daughter, and that my marriage had ended. I explained that Utah was very family-oriented and that I felt out of place there. He asked me why I didn't consider my daughter and myself a family.

"I guess I do," I said. "But the rest of Utah doesn't consider us a family."

"Actually, I just moved here myself," he said. "I've been living in Philadelphia and going to school at Temple, and now I've moved out here to go to law school." He had a distinctive way of speaking, not really an eastern accent, but more like a British one. His name, he said, was Ted Bundy.

I knew when I first looked at him, before we had even danced, that he was a cut above the rest of the crowd. His slacks and turtleneck certainly weren't from J.C. Penney, and the way he moved projected confidence. He seemed to be in control of his world.

Sitting across the table from him I was surprised at how easy he was to talk to and how easily we laughed together. He had a smile that made me smile back and beautiful clear blue eyes that lit up when he smiled. He had thick eyelashes, a strong jawline, rich curly hair, and a nice body. When he told me he was only twenty-three, I couldn't believe it.

He said he didn't realize he had been looking sad; he was just thinking about leaving. The couple at the next table got up to go and offered us their unfinished pitcher of beer. I said I was never one to let good beer go flat. Ted wanted to know where I'd been around Seattle. "You haven't been to the public market? We should go there sometime. You'll love it." The chemistry between us was incredible. As I watched his handsome face while he went on about places to go and things to see, I was already planning the wedding and naming the kids. He was telling me that he missed having a kitchen because he loved to cook. Perfect. My Prince.

The pitcher was empty, and the crowd was moving on. I invited Ted to come for coffee with my friends and he said, "Sure." Since he didn't have a car, he would come in mine along with Angie and a couple of other people. When we stepped outside, the rush of night air made me realize how drunk I was. We couldn't find the cafe we were headed for, and as the glow began to dim, Angie and the others decided to go home. When they got out of the car at her house, Ted moved into the driver's seat and drove me to the babysitter's house to pick up Molly. The babysitter was wearing nothing but overalls, and when she bent over you could see right down to her navel. I was embarrassed, but Ted didn't seem to notice. He scooped up the sleeping Molly and carried her to the car. I drove and Ted held Molly on his lap.

Ted was doing most of the talking now, and I was beginning to feel very sick. He was writing a book on Vietnam explaining how the cultural differences between Americans and Vietnamese con-tributed to the war. I was a little surprised and a little skeptical, but I was mostly concentrating on driving the car and not throwing up.

The closest parking space was two blocks from my apartment. Ted carried Molly in and gently put her to bed on the couch.

"I don't think I can drive you home," I said. "Why don't you just stay here?"

I was so sick, all I could do was take my shoes off and fall into bed. I remember Ted, still dressed, lying down next to me, then the room turning wildly. I hung one leg over the edge of the bed and put my foot on the floor to make it stop spinning. Then I slept, restlessly.

I knew Ted was up and walking around the apartment part of the night. Once, I opened my eyes and saw him standing next to my dresser, looking at my bottles of perfume and things. I wished I hadn't left my birth control pills out, but I wasn't awake long enough to imagine what he must be thinking.

— CHAPTER THREE —

It was seven o'clock in the morning and I felt as if I hadn't slept at all. I could hear Ted moving around in the kitchen. Never in my life had I brought a man home from a bar. Was this what city life was all about? My head throbbed as I got out of bed, still dressed in yesterday's clothes, and staggered into the living room.

Ted was coming out of the kitchen with a cup of coffee for me. Oh God. I hadn't remembered how gorgeous he was. He didn't look as if he'd slept in his clothes. He put his finger to his lips and pointed to the sleeping Molly. He didn't need to shush me because I couldn't think of a thing to say.

"How do you feel?" he whispered as we headed back to the bedroom.

"Awful. Incredibly awful." I fumbled in my purse for aspirin.

"You'll feel better after you eat," he said. "If it's all right with you, I'll scramble some eggs and make some toast."

"I'm not a breakfast person, really." The idea of food made me sick.

"I've already started," he confessed.

I took a fast shower, put on fresh clothes, and joined him at the table. Molly would be awake soon and I needed to be together when I introduced her to this man that I didn't even know. I had no idea how to behave.

Molly and I had planned to go for a ferry ride across Puget Sound. Ted hinted that he'd like to come along, but I ignored the hint and offered to drop him off at his house in the University District. Too much was happening too fast.

When the ferry whistle blew, I thought my head would split. I couldn't look at the water slipping past beneath us without getting dizzy. Molly pressed her face to the window while I sat clutching a cup of coffee. I had really blown it, I thought. Picking up men in bars was not my style. Yet I had taken Ted home without a second thought after knowing him for two or three hours.

I wondered about him. He acted as though it wasn't an out-of-the-ordinary experience for him, yet he seemed so classy, above that sort of encounter. What would he think of me? What sort of mother would take a strange man home in front of her child?

Two hours' worth of Puget Sound scenery was lost on me. By the time the boat eased into the Seattle dock, I had decided that I never wanted to see Ted again. I hoped that the memory of last night would somehow disappear.

Ted called that night, as cheerful as he'd been in the morning. He wanted to know how we enjoyed the ferry ride and joked about how drunk I'd been and my terrible hangover. But I was distant, still humiliated, and we chatted only a few minutes.

Monday came and I couldn't stop thinking about what had happened. I was really attracted to this man—not just a little—but I wished I had met him differently.

Tuesday, someone from the University Personnel Office called my office to verify that I was working there. It seemed a little odd at the time. As I left work and headed for my car, I looked up to see Ted coming towards me across the parking lot.

"Well, hello," I blurted out, "I was just thinking about you." I blushed and felt ridiculous: I hadn't thought about much else for the last three days.

We fell into talking as easily as we had at the tavern. We agreed on dinner at my place, he suggested steaks and wine, and I tossed him the car keys. We went to a supermarket I hadn't discovered before. It was huge and spotlessly clean, with wide aisles and no long lines at the cash registers. I learned later that it was the classiest supermarket in town. The mom-and-pop store near my apartment was a grimy little place that did most of its business in Thunderbird.

Ted knew a lot about food and wine. He chose the steaks, a loaf of French bread, and salad greens, then took me across the street to a wine store. "This should be good," he said, taking a bottle of French red wine off the shelf. I was impressed by any wine that had a cork in the bottle.

We collected Molly from the daycare center and went home to cook. I was impressed with Ted's skill in the kitchen; he had left it spotless after Sunday's breakfast, and now he took command.

"You wouldn't happen to have any fresh garlic, would you?" he asked.

"Oh sure," I said and got it out of the cupboard. *At last*, I thought to myself happily, *I finally did something right*. I put the bread in the oven and made the salad while we talked nonstop about ourselves, the city, politics—all the things people talk about when they are first getting to know each other.

Molly was testing the water, demanding a lot of attention. Ted told me he hadn't been around little kids much, but he was charming with her. After dinner he asked her if she had a favorite book he could read to her. She loved stories, and she ran and got *Teddy Bear of Bumpkin Hollow*.

"Ah, yes," Ted said. "I know this story well. *Freddy Bear of Bumpkin Hollow*."

"No, no," giggled Molly. "It's *TEDDY Bear of Bumpkin Hollow*!"

"I see," Ted said. "*Teddy Bear of Pumpkin Hollow*."

"*Bumpkin*," said Molly. And so it went, Molly hanging on Ted's every word, waiting to catch his silly mistakes.

We put Molly to sleep in my bed, and as we did the dishes we talked again about the Northwest. Ted was not from the East Coast, as I had assumed, but from Tacoma, a city about thirty miles south of Seattle. He knew the region well and was delighted at how enchanted I was with his native territory. He wanted to show me all his favorite places.

When Molly was finally asleep and the bottle of wine was almost empty, he asked me if I would spend the weekend with him in Vancouver, British Columbia. I said yes. He kissed me goodnight and went home, but when we kissed it was clear that we both wanted more.

I called Angie with the good news. I tried to maintain a little bit of cool; I didn't want to set myself up for a big fall, but it is hard to be cool when you're wearing an ear-to-ear grin. Angie would be away, but she said I could leave Molly with her roommates.

Friday morning Ted came to take us to work and daycare so he could take the car to the gas station to fill it up and check the tires, the oil, and whatever else. In a corduroy sports coat and a tie, he looked like a young man going off to a law office to research an important case. The day flew by.

I was excited, but I was also scared. Would I be nervous and tongue-tied during the three-hour drive? I needn't have worried. He talked about growing up in Tacoma, becoming a Boy Scout and selling American flags door-to-door. He said that when he owned a house, he was going to put a flagpole out front and fly the American flag every day, not just on holidays. I didn't know if he was serious or not.

We talked about Vietnam. My brother had been there, and I had been afraid he was going to die there. I didn't think America belonged in Vietnam. Ted and I agreed that the overkill—the use of napalm and bombs—made it plain that we were out to destroy Vietnam rather than save it. Ted told me that he had not been drafted because he was 4-F. He had broken his ankle when he was back East, and it hadn't healed right, but the draft board in Tacoma didn't think a broken ankle should keep a young man out of the service, so he was having a running battle with them.

We arrived in Vancouver about seven-thirty. It was almost as beautiful as Seattle at night. Ted had wanted to stay at the Hotel Vancouver, an elegant old hotel in the heart of the city, but he found that they didn't have any rooms so we drove down the block to the Devonshire. I stayed in the car when he went in, wondering how he was going to register. Mr. and Mrs. T. R. Bundy had a nice ring to it.

We walked back to the Hotel Vancouver for dinner in a huge, high-ceilinged, ornate restaurant with enormous chandeliers. I was in awe. Afterwards, we went dancing at Oilcan Harry's, a lively place with go-go dancers and a peculiar mix of hippies, straight young people, and older businessmen types.

We danced some, but mostly we sat at the table drinking Scotch and water and taking the whole scene in. The music was so loud we had to yell over it. It was also hot and crowded. Soon Ted leaned over and whispered in my ear, "Let's go." The cool air outside felt good. Ted turned to me, put both arms around me, and gave me a long, long kiss.

"I have been wanting to do this since I met you six years ago," he said. "Or was it just six days ago?" He kissed me again. We were oblivious to the people detouring around us on the sidewalk. "If we keep this up," he said, "we will have to call an aid car to take us back to the hotel."

We got back to the hotel, walking some and kissing a lot. As we walked through the lobby we tried to look calm. Heaven forbid that the desk clerk or bell captain should know what we were about to do. But as we got into the elevator, I began to get cold feet. Did I really want this gorgeous guy to see my body with its stretch marks, small breasts, and the extra five pounds I had been carrying around since Molly was born?

Ted apparently felt no hesitation, nor did he sense mine. In our room he put his arms around me and began kissing me; then the chemistry took over. We made love as though this would be the last time we would ever see each other, as if we were trying to get enough of each other to last a lifetime.

I felt good next to him. He ran his fingertips over my back. I wondered if he enjoyed our lovemaking as much as I did. I had made love with two other men besides my husband, both after my divorce. For different reasons, neither time had been satisfying. This was different. We made love again and finally fell asleep about four in the morning.

We lingered over breakfast in our room, sitting by the window looking out at the street and the large fountain below. We talked more about ourselves, about my life in Utah and Ted's future as a lawyer. I told him about my high school sweetheart. He told me about an old flame named Susan. He had met her while living in a University of Washington dormitory. She was slender, pretty, intelligent, from a wealthy San Francisco family. She eventually went back home. Ted had followed her there and enrolled in a summer course in Chinese at Stanford, but, he said, they had drifted apart. She had a life of her own apart from him, and he seemed to feel it was her wealth that shut him out. That surprised me. He was always so well dressed, and he seemed so at ease in these luxurious surroundings.

Finally, we went out to look at the city. Vancouver was even more cosmopolitan than Seattle. We roamed through the large Chinatown, up through a German neighborhood, and past quaint tea shops. We walked with our arms around each other, moving together in perfect rhythm. I was light-headed.

The drive back to Seattle Saturday afternoon was filled with unending conversation. We covered religion (neither of us was an active churchgoer), drugs (neither of us smoked dope), TV (neither of us had any use for it). We still had so much to cover we didn't want to part. We stopped in Seattle and bought food for dinner before we picked up Molly. She had a lot to tell us and pictures she had drawn to show us. Ted had brought some Canadian candy back for her.

After we got Molly to bed, we settled down for more wine and conversation. Ted liked what he called my "small-town perspective." He thought it was less cynical than most city people's. He laughed when I talked about how painful my shyness was and how my neck and face got covered with red blotches.

We made love. "Do you want me to go home?" he asked. I had mixed feelings about that. It was wonderful to lie next to him, but after my divorce I had often told myself that I would never subject Molly to a string of male overnight guests. I had to teach by example, not words. On the other hand, I really wanted him to stay.

"Maybe if we got dressed before she got up," I said. We left the matter dangling as we drifted off to sleep.

On Sunday, Ted showed Molly and me his room in the University District. In an immaculately kept old rooming house owned by an elderly German couple, Ernst and Freda, Ted had a big corner room on the second floor, with enormous windows and a high ceiling. The hardwood floors were covered with an old, dusty-pink-patterned carpet. Everything was orderly and spotless—a starched doily lay across the top of his dresser. Ted introduced me to his roommate, a Boston fern that sat in the corner where the windows met. He called the plant Fern and fussed over it. He had a small stereo that he kept tuned to Seattle's classical music station. The whole place had an airy charm that reminded me of houses I'd seen on a trip to Europe when I was in high school. I thought it suited him perfectly.

Soon we began spending most of our time together. He had a temporary job with a messenger firm that delivered legal papers. I thought he had told me he was a law student the night we met, but in fact, he was waiting to start law school the next quarter.

I was amazed and pleased at how much Ted liked our domestic scene. He seemed hungry for family life. He took Molly and me out to all of his favorite places: the public market; the main street of the University District called "the Ave," where we browsed through used book and record stores; the International District, where we ate Chinese food and Ted tried out his limited Chinese on the patient waiters.

We made love every chance we got. I had never felt this close to any man before.

I had resolved, I told him, that I would never get involved with another student. I wanted to be with someone more established, someone who could support me while I raised the kids. "And yet the thought of losing you, of not being with you. . . ."

"I know," he said. "I feel the same way. But it's as if we knew each other before in some former life. We fit together so well in so many ways. We fill in all the gaps for each other. I look back on my life before I met you and it seems it was terribly empty. I love you more than you know."

We did fit together well. I believed that the man should be the leader in a relationship, and Ted liked to lead. I liked his protectiveness of me and Molly, both emotionally and physically. I was naive about what goes on in the city, and sometimes I took unnecessary risks.

One night when Ted came over after dinner, I told him that Molly and I had stopped at Volunteer Park on the way home from work to swing, and that we'd had the park practically to ourselves.

He was horrified. "Don't you realize how isolated you are there in case of trouble?"

"Trouble? What kind of trouble?"

"You name it and you can probably find it in Volunteer Park, especially at dusk. If you want to play in a park, come get me first. You understand?"

I nodded sheepishly. I hadn't used my head.

CHAPTER FOUR

I liked my job, but the eight-to-five grind wore me down, and when I got tired, I would get short-tempered with Molly. Then I would feel guilty about the kind of mother I was, and then a homesick feeling would set in. Ted helped protect me from the "whip lady" who lived inside me, who was always telling me I should be a better mother, should work harder, should have more energy. He believed I was doing okay with Molly and with my job, too. His opinion meant a lot to me.

I had long since confessed to him that I was a secretary, but he liked to hear about my job and told me he thought my work was important. My story about making heart valves had become a joke between us; every Sunday night Ted would say, "Well, you'd better get to sleep early so you'll be rested up for making those heart valves tomorrow."

Talking and eating and taking care of Molly and sleeping together all flowed along so effortlessly that we had become a family. Ted planned special outings that he knew would be fun for Molly—trips to Green Lake to feed bread to the ducks, or visits to the zoo. As we walked along, Molly would grab both of our hands and shout, "Swing me! Swing me!" I seemed to get tired of this much quicker than Ted or Molly, but when I wouldn't play anymore, they didn't care. Ted would swing her by an arm and a leg until they were both dizzy. At home, the two of them would get into tickle fights on the floor. Molly would holler, "Save me, Mom, save me!" and then we'd all roll around on the floor, laughing and tickling until someone, usually me, would call for a truce.

On Saturday mornings, Molly and Ted would watch cartoons together and let me sleep in. Their favorite was Dudley Doright and the Mounties. Dudley had a girlfriend named Nell whom he saved from villains who routinely tied her to railroad tracks. Ted could mimic Dudley perfectly, and he would call Molly "Nell." Together, "Dudley and Nell" would fix breakfast and bring it to me in bed.

One weeknight in November, Ted took us to dinner at his parents' house in Tacoma. He had told me that Tacoma was a boring, ugly town. I didn't think it looked bad, but the smell got to me—a smell of rotten eggs that I first noticed ten full miles north of town. Ted said it came from a pulp mill and was known locally as "The Tacoma Aroma."

I was nervous about meeting Ted's folks. I was sure that being divorced and having a child were two strikes against me, and I expected them to be wealthy. But they lived in a warm and homey two-story colonial house, to which they had recently moved. Ted had grown up in a house that he hated because his room in the basement had never been finished and it embarrassed him to bring friends home, he said. I met his four younger brothers and sisters, who all still lived at home, and I hit it off with his father.

Johnnie Bundy was a cook at an army hospital. He was from the Ozarks, and he was full of long stories about scrambling eggs for five hundred people and about cars that broke down. He talked a blue streak in a southern accent, and I was happy to listen. He was open and friendly, and he made me feel welcome.

Louise, Ted's mother, was a secretary at their Methodist Church. She was friendly, too, but in a more formal way. Ted assured me on the way home that they had liked Molly and me.

"As much as they liked Susan?" I asked. The memory of his slender, pretty, intelligent, wealthy ex-girlfriend was still with me.

"They probably liked you more," he said laughing.

I realized now that my family was more affluent than Ted's. His finances were the same as most of the students I knew: He was broke most of the time. Not long after our deluxe weekend in Vancouver, Ted took me to dinner at an expensive restaurant overlooking Puget Sound. Later, he confessed that he had spent his last dollar on that meal, and that we would have had to wash dishes if I had ordered another drink. We laughed about it, and I was all the more flattered that he had taken me there. Even on the night we met in the Sandpiper Tavern, he finally confessed, the reason he was sitting at the table looking so dejected was that he had run out of money for beer.

Yet neither of us doubted that wealth was in Ted's future. He was marked for success. I was perfectly happy to go places with him in my car, to pay for the gas, and to pay for the food he ate at my house. I was sure it would all even out eventually.

Molly and I were planning to fly home to Utah to spend Christmas with my folks. A couple of Angie's friends were driving to Utah for the holidays, and it didn't take much to persuade Ted to go with them. They had trouble getting through the snowbound mountain passes, and when they pulled up at my parents' house late on Christmas Eve, Mom and Dad had gone to bed. It was cold and clear, and the ground was covered with snow. Ted couldn't believe how clear the sky was and how many stars there were. We rolled in the snow and washed each other's faces in it. I showed him my old bedroom where Molly and I would be sleeping, and the guest room where he would sleep. We snickered about what saints we were pretending to be. I wouldn't dream of telling my parents about our sleeping arrangements in Seattle.

When Ted met my parents in the morning, he liked them, and they liked him. He talked politics and football with my dad. I always thought of my dad as quiet and reserved, but he and Ted talked on for hours. My mom never lets anyone help in the kitchen, so Ted didn't ask to help—he just did. She loves to tell jokes, and Ted was the perfect audience. The two of them laughed and cooked Christmas dinner together and kept the rest of us out of the kitchen. Later, we all went out together to visit family friends, and Ted seemed to fit in wherever he went. It was a relief to me to be with him and let him carry the conversation. Late in the day, he called his family in Tacoma to wish them a Merry Christmas.

My folks were pleased with Ted, my mother's only criticism being that she thought he was too hard on Molly; but she was a grand-mother and even I thought she spoiled Molly sometimes.

Mom and Dad wanted to keep Molly for an extra week, and she couldn't have been more excited. Ted drove back with Angie's friends, and the next day I flew back to Seattle alone to find the dreariest of the gray winter rain. But Ted came over that night and the weather didn't matter at all.

Ted and I had a week alone to spend any way we wanted. For the first time, we could spend nights at his place. I liked being there, surrounded by his things. I laughed at the Styrofoam, imitation-straw souvenir hat he kept from the 1968 Rockefeller campaign, but Ted was proud of it. He had gone to the Republican Convention in Miami to support Rockefeller. All that hoopla might look silly from the outside, he said, but he found himself caught up in the excitement of the convention.

Conservative as he was, Ted was sympathetic to some of the student demonstrations on campus. He was against the war in Viet-nam and critical of the university as an institution. The campus was in constant turmoil in those days. Ted came to my office one day, out of breath, to tell me that Thompson Hall had been occupied by protesters who alleged that the building was the center of CIA activity on campus. We went out to watch. The police had put up barricades across the street, and the whole scene was unreal, like a movie set.

"They haven't trashed anything," Ted said. "They pulled it off; they've got the building, and it was completely nonviolent."

This was a long way from Ogden. I didn't even know what "trashed" meant.

But as sophisticated as Ted was, he had one hangup that surprised me. Not long after we started spending time together, he came over one night and said he had something very important to tell me, something that might change my opinion of him. Shaking with nervousness, he told me that he was illegitimate. His mother gave birth to him in a home for unwed mothers in the East, he said, and they moved to Tacoma to live with relatives when he was very small. Then she married Johnnie Bundy and had four more children. Johnnie Bundy had adopted him, but Ted knew nothing about it until he was a teenager.

It had come as a terrible shock. A cousin had been teasing him about it, and Ted had refused to believe it. The cousin had taken Ted up to the attic and showed him proof: his birth certificate. Ted was upset by his cousin's cruelty and furious with his mother because she had left him unprepared for humiliation at the hands of his cousin. "She never even had the decency to tell me herself," he said bitterly. He asked if I thought he should confront his mother about it.

I told him no. I could sympathize with her. She had made a mistake when she was young, as I had, but had overcome it and had gone on to make a life for herself. It could not have been easy that many years ago—harder, I was sure, than it was for me when I was pregnant with Molly. "I'm sure it's a source of a lot of pain for her," I said, "and that's probably why she didn't talk about it. It's not important anymore. What's important is that you've got a lot going for you. I love you because you're wonderful."

Ted put his head in his hands and cried.

It bothered him that his family was middle class. He was ambitious and wanted to be better than that. He liked the fact that my father was a successful doctor. But to me, at least, his family's status didn't seem to be a major problem; Ted was very fond of them, and success would be all the more satisfying to him if he made it on his own.

Our more immediate concern was apartment hunting. Ted thought my apartment was unsafe, bad for Molly, and much too small, and he was right on all counts. He helped me look, and in January 1970, for not much more than I was already paying, we found a wonderful duplex in north Seattle near Green Lake and its surrounding park. It had all the luxuries I had been missing: a lawn for Molly to play on, a washer and dryer, a second bedroom, big closets, and a kitchen you could turn around in. Ted negotiated with my old landlord and got my deposit returned, even though I had not stayed for the six months minimum I had agreed to.

The Green Lake place was like heaven. As the weather got warmer, we carried our table outside for dinner once in a while, and Ted would pick flowers for the table and light candles in the dusk. We fell into a new routine: Ted kept his room in the University District, but he spent most nights with us. He drove Molly to daycare and me to work every morning and kept the car during the day. The closet filled up with his clothes.

I had never been so happy, but it bothered me to be practically living with a man I wasn't married to. I wasn't sure anymore what Molly understood, but when we went places together, people often assumed that Ted was her father. Ted and I had been talking about our future together almost since we met, how when we were rich, we would drive a Mercedes and buy a beach place on Puget Sound. We talked about *when* we were married, but we never actually talked about *getting* married. I figured now was the time. We were playing house and enjoying it. Why not make it legal and honest? I didn't like not being able to be open with my parents about the exact nature of my relationship with Ted, and I felt that it wasn't fair to Molly to have this man around who wasn't really her dad. There wasn't even a word for what he was in relation to us.

When I talked about him to others, I never knew what to call him. *Boyfriend* seemed to be too high school. *Lover* was true but not socially acceptable. I wanted to be able to refer to *my husband, Ted.* When I talked with him about it, he agreed that now was the time to do it. If he was reluctant in any way, he didn't show it. One day in February, I took time off from work to get the license and Angie met us at the courthouse on her lunch hour to be our witness. She also loaned us five dollars for the license.

I wrote to my parents and told them the good news. They were very pleased. Ted held off telling his parents. Then one Sunday we went to Tacoma for dinner. It was a happy day, but dinner passed without a word about our plans from Ted. About five o'clock, when it was almost time to head back to Seattle, he and his mom disappeared. I knew he must be discussing our marriage plans with her and wondered why I wasn't included. When they came back in, Mrs. Bundy gave me a hug and said she wished happiness for us, but I had the feeling that she didn't believe I was good enough for Ted. On the ride home, Ted told me she thought we should wait until he graduated. I thought that was stupid. If we got married now, I could help put Ted through law school. I liked the idea of working toward a goal together.

A few days later at Northgate Mall we passed a jewelry store. "Let's go in and look at rings," I suggested.

"What's the point in looking?" he said. "We can't afford anything but a plain band. Hell, we probably can't even afford that."

"It doesn't hurt to dream," I said. We went inside the store, but he looked at watch bands while I looked at rings. When a salesperson came over, Ted wouldn't say anything. I was getting angry, and he was acting so nervous that I was afraid the jeweler might think we were casing the place. "Let's go," I said, trying to control my voice. When we were outside, I said, "Let's stop at the liquor store and get some Scotch. I could use a drink." I was scared. I wanted desperately for things to work out as I planned.

A few days later, Ted and I were walking from my office to the parking lot. My parents were coming soon for a visit, and I hoped we would get married while they were here. I told Ted that we should move his clothes out of my closet before they came because I didn't want them to know that we were practically living together.

Ted thought that was childish. "You're a grown woman, Liz. You have a daughter of your own and a life of your own. For Godsake, grow up!" When we got to the car, he put his briefcase on the hood, opened the case, took out the marriage license, and said, "If you're that hung up on what your parents think, then you're not ready to get married. Let's forget the whole thing." He tore the license up in little pieces and threw them on the ground. Then he turned and walked away.

I stared at his back, not believing what had happened. I looked at the pieces of the marriage license on the ground as if they were vomit, sick of myself for pushing and pushing until I had pushed the man I loved right out of my life.

I stopped at the liquor store before I picked Molly up, agonizing because everything I did turned to worms.

I tried to get Molly fed and into bed without her knowing how upset I was. She wanted to know where Ted was. "Busy," was all I could get out. After she was asleep, I poured myself a drink and sat down to figure out what had happened and what the next step was. I called Angie and unloaded on her.

"Just because Ted doesn't want to get married doesn't mean he doesn't love you," she said. "The important thing is that you guys are happy together. Who is getting married these days, anyway? When he's ready, he'll marry you." Angie's words and the Scotch made me feel better.

As I was getting ready for bed, I heard Ted's key in the lock. I was ashamed that my face was all swollen from crying. I didn't want him to know how important marriage was to me. If I could be casual about it and act as if it was no big deal, maybe I wouldn't drive him away.

He came into the bedroom and put his arms around me. "I don't want to sleep alone tonight," he said and kissed me on the forehead. "I really do love you."

CHAPTER FIVE

Coming so close to losing Ted made me realize how very, very much I loved him. I found the idea of working and putting him through law school appealing, but I could understand that taking on family responsibilities before he even started law school might be a real drag for him.

Ted planned to start law school the winter quarter of 1970, but Temple University did not get his transcripts out in time, so he was held up for another quarter. I kept reminding him to check up on his application to be sure everything was in order, but he regarded my reminders as nagging, and whenever I tried to talk about law school, he changed the subject or brushed my questions aside with vague answers. When I began to realize the futility of nagging, I made the decision to shut up about it.

Spring quarter of 1970 started and still no word about law school. "There seems to be some problem with my transcripts from Temple," Ted told me.

"Why didn't you call them?" I asked.

"I guess there are other problems," he said. "It's too late to do anything about it now."

I couldn't figure it out. What other problems? I couldn't keep from brooding about it. One day I dialed the law school telephone number a couple of times but hung up each time before anyone answered. What could I say?

Finally, I called the admissions office. I began to explain about my friend who was supposed to start law school winter quarter, when I was interrupted by the woman I was speaking to.

"All law school students start at the beginning of fall quarter," she said. "There are no exceptions."

There must be some mistake, I told myself. Then it dawned on me whose mistake it was. I was livid by the time Ted showed up at my office to take me home.

"How could you lie to me?" I asked him.

"I am going to start school for sure this summer," he said, "but I still have two years of undergraduate work left. I can understand if you can't live with it."

His calmness made me feel like a raving maniac. He'd lied to me, but hadn't I lied to him the night we met in the tavern and I told him about making heart valves? But this lie about law school had gone on for six months. I had told everybody I knew about my law student boyfriend. Maybe I had made such a big deal out of it that it was impossible for Ted to tell me the truth. I could understand his wanting to be someone he wasn't. I had those feelings, too. Maybe I made him feel that he wasn't good enough as he was. There was no doubt in my mind that he would be a successful lawyer someday; it would just take a little longer than I'd counted on. I wasn't about to give him up over this.

Ted took classes in the summer quarter and got a part-time job in a medical supply house close to my work. It was a happy time. Some days he'd pick up a submarine sandwich and a quart of beer and join me for lunch on a secluded patch of campus lawn. After work I'd walk over to his job and pick him up, and we'd walk up the Ave, window-shopping. Then we'd pick up Molly at daycare and go to my place and fix dinner. On hot summer days we'd take inner tubes and go swimming at Green Lake before dinner or go wading after it got dark.

We drove to Utah at the end of summer. The Wasatch Mountains were more beautiful than ever. Ted and I went horseback riding in the foothills where I had played as a kid, went fishing in Wyoming with Molly and my parents, and drank beer in local hangouts. One night in Wyoming, Ted put on his cowboy boots and borrowed my dad's cowboy hat and we walked down the highway to town. Ted couldn't resist lying down in the middle of the still-warm pavement to celebrate the peace and quiet.

We went back to Seattle, leaving Molly with her grandparents. We spent two weeks going out drinking and dancing. One night, we stopped by a secondhand store run by a friend of Ted's. The friend was just closing up and invited us into the back of the store where he lived. It was like stepping into the 1930s, with period furniture and dance band records. The pipe and the hash he pulled out brought us back to 1970.

I had smoked dope maybe three times before and had never even got a buzz on. For this people risked being arrested? But this time when I stood up, my legs felt like rubber, I fell against Ted, and we collapsed laughing into an overstuffed chair. Every time we tried to get up, we collapsed, laughing hysterically. We stumbled out the door, tripped, and fell into a big cardboard packing crate. I wanted to sleep there all night, but Ted said we had to go home to make love. Why couldn't we make love in the packing crate? Every time he tried to explain, we would laugh so hard we would cry. The thought of food finally moved us. We went to the hole-in-the-wall cafe on the Ave that was noted for having the greasiest food in Seattle, possibly in the nation. We had ended up like many drunks there, gobbling up greaseburgers to soak up the alcohol.

When the high faded, Ted talked about his friend at the second-hand store. "He's real stupid taking such chances with dope. He just got paroled from prison." I was surprised.

"He used to have another store," Ted explained. "He would break into houses, steal stuff, and sell it in his store. He got caught."

"How do you know him?" I asked.

"I used to live with him and his girlfriend."

"When?"

"Just for a couple of months. When I worked for Safeway." I knew that Ted had stolen some of his textbooks, and soon after we met, he had shown me a new pair of ski boots that he said he had taken from an unlocked display case at the student union building. He was pleased with himself and said that if he hadn't taken them, someone else would have. Now I wondered if he had been involved with his friend with the secondhand store. It was out of character for Ted, with his law-and-order views, even to know a convicted burglar. Stealing textbooks was so common it didn't shock me, but I considered it a dumb risk for someone who wanted to earn fame and fortune as an attorney.

Summer gave way to autumn which gave way to winter. We passed our first anniversary; Molly and I went home to Utah for Christmas without Ted and stayed till New Year's Day. I spent New Year's Eve with my high school girlfriends, getting blasted and telling them about my wonderful boyfriend. At midnight, I went outside, lay in the snow, and shouted drunkenly for all the world to hear, "I'm in love!" We celebrated Christmas with Ted when we got back. He had put up the prettiest tree I had ever seen and gave Molly some wonderful presents, including two Christmas kittens.

But around March of 1971 I was getting antsy again—I thought Ted and I were so comfortable, we would never get married if I didn't do something. "I've been thinking," I told him, "that since we're not married and we don't have any plans, how do you feel about dating other people?"

"What have you got in mind?" he asked.

I wanted to say, "To push you off your duff, Dumbo," but instead

I told him that a guy at work had been asking me out, that I told this guy I had a boyfriend, and he asked me what kind of commitment we had, and I didn't know what to tell him. I put the accent on "commitment."

"I don't want to date anyone else," he said, "but I know it's not fair to ask you not to. Go ahead and go."

This wasn't what I'd planned. *Well, the hell with you*, I thought. There was no guy at work, but I got Angie to line me up with one of her boyfriend's friends. Ted didn't seem to care when I told him I was going out on Friday night, but I was a nervous wreck by the time my date picked me up.

We went with Angie and her date to a tavern called The Walrus to drink and dance. I was having a miserable time, when Angie grabbed me and pulled my ear close to her mouth.

"You've got company," she said.

I followed her eyes to the far wall and there stood Ted, glaring at me. I was furious at him for acting like he didn't care a bit, and then following me. I marched over to him and demanded that he leave. He was shaking like a leaf and insisted that I leave with him.

"Are you crazy?" I said. "You treat me like you don't care about me. You let our relationship drag on for over a year and a half with absolutely no kind of commitment, and now you want me to leave with you. No thanks!"

When I got back to the table I looked back, and Ted was gone. So was the party, and everybody wanted to go. In the car my date was all over me. When we pulled up in front of my place, there was Ted, pacing back and forth on the sidewalk. I stormed in with Ted at my heels.

"Did you have a good time?" he started in. "Is that what you want, to go drinking and dancing every Friday night?"

"What's the choice?'" I wanted to know. "Wait around for you until I'm eighty-five? I'm going to be twenty-six next month. I want to get on with my life."

"I know, I know," he said. I thought he might cry. "You deserve someone who can make you happy, someone who has 'made it' already. I love you so much. Tonight, when I saw you with someone else, I got so scared. I want to spend my whole life with you, and when we are eighty-five, we'll laugh and tell our grandchildren about the night Grandpa followed Grandma out on her date."

In May, Molly turned five and had her first real birthday party. Ted made a big Happy Birthday sign and hung it across the living room. He blew up balloons with his bicycle pump, and he made a chocolate cake and decorated it himself.

In July, I found a two-bedroom apartment in the University District, closer to Ted's place. It was the main floor of an old house, dirty and cramped, but it came furnished with Oriental rugs over hardwood floors, a wonderful old mahogany dining table with velvet-cushioned chairs, a fireplace with built-in bookshelves on each side, beamed ceilings, and a built-in hutch with leaded-glass doors. It was on a tree-lined street just north of the campus where Ted and I had walked often, dreaming of how nice it would be to live there. Ted bought an old-fashioned hide-a-bed for fifty dollars. On rainy nights we would build a fire in the fireplace and fall asleep in the hide-a-bed watching the embers glowing.

But soon, the pattern of our life changed. Our places were so close that he began walking home late some nights instead of spending the whole night with me. We still ate dinner together, but sometimes he just didn't show up. At other times, he would show up when I wasn't expecting him. Our lives were out of sync.

He was busier at school. He would graduate in nine months and he had to take the Law School Admission Test (the LSAT) before Christmas. I knew he had a lot on his mind, so I tried to keep busy without him. I signed up for a night class in oceanography, and Ted babysat for me while I went to class.

That fall, Ted took the LSAT and worried that he hadn't done well. When his test scores came back low, I was surprised. He was intelligent, but he couldn't seem to produce well on tests. He took the test a second time, and when the scores came back about the same as the first time, he was devastated. He had applied to six law schools and had outstanding letters of recommendation from his professors. Maybe the LSAT scores wouldn't stop him. His first choice was Hastings College of the Law in San Francisco; his last choice the University of Utah.

Early in 1972, my doctor advised me to give my body a rest from birth control pills. He stressed the importance of finding an alternative method of birth control before I stopped taking the pill. Ted and I discussed the alternatives, but none of them sounded very appealing, so we decided we would just be very careful. We had a good sex life, still exciting, but without the urgency of the early days, so we thought we could manage by abstaining during my fertile days. We didn't anticipate the "forbidden fruit" aspect of abstaining that would make indulging all the more exciting. Soon I was getting up in the middle of the night to go to the bathroom, and my breasts were swelling.

Both of us knew it would be impossible to have a baby now. He was going to start law school in the fall, and I needed to be able to work to put him through. I was distraught. I knew I was going to terminate the pregnancy as soon as I could. Ted, on the other hand, was pleased with himself. He had fathered a baby. I didn't want to hear about it. I didn't want to think about what I was going to do. I wanted to sleep most of the time, while Ted did most of the cooking and looked after Molly.

As soon as a doctor confirmed what we already knew, I made an appointment for an abortion, which had just been legalized in Washington State. It was awful. Ted took me home and put me to bed. He lay down beside me and talked about the day when I wouldn't have to work, and we would have lots of kids. He fixed me food which I couldn't eat and did all he could to comfort me. Within a few days I was feeling better and determined never to think of it again.

When the University of Utah Law School sent Ted an acceptance letter, he was ecstatic. Feeling sure that this was only the beginning of his acceptances, he wrote and declined the offer. Then five rejections arrived in a row. Now Ted cried and it was my turn to offer comfort. It took him a couple of weeks to get back on his feet, but he decided that a year's worth of work experience would look good on his record, and he would just have to reapply next year.

— CHAPTER SIX —

In June 1972, Ted graduated from the University of Washington with honors. His family came to Seattle for the celebration, the graduation ceremonies, and then a salmon dinner at my place. Ted proposed a toast to me for my help in getting him through school. His mother wanted to know what I had done to help. Had I typed his papers? Didn't she know I was practically supporting him? As a graduation present, I gave him a yellow rubber raft.

Molly went to Utah to stay with my parents later in June, and Ted took a fulltime job for the summer at Harborview Hospital's Mental Health Center. I spent the July 4 weekend in Utah, but Molly didn't come back with me. I was lonely and everything seemed to make me sad. The day I got back, Ted asked me if I wanted to go out the next night, a Friday, but I was so tired I said I didn't know. The next day I felt a lot better and called Ted at his job to tell him that I did want to go out after all.

He stammered and hemmed and hawed and finally told me that he had a date.

"What? A date? With who?"

"A woman I work with. Remember, I asked you first. . . ."

"Tell me you're kidding," I pleaded. "Please don't do this to me." I slammed down the phone and waited for him to call back. But he didn't. I told my boss I had to leave. I rode my bike home, crying all the way and talking out loud to myself, telling myself it wasn't true. I took my bike into my apartment and threw it on the floor. I let out a scream. "You asshole!" I shouted. "You fucker! You made me kill my baby for you and your goddamn career. You're a miserable son-of-a-bitch, Ted Bundy. I hate you!"

Then I started in on myself, "God, you're stupid Liz. You're a goddamn stupid idiot. A goddamn ugly pig. What did you think he would do? Love you and cherish you? He's just used you and now he's through with you."

I poured myself a glass of Scotch and drank it straight. It burned and tasted awful, but I deserved to be burned. I prayed the phone would ring. Or that he would knock on the door, put his arms around me, take my pain away. I poured another drink. I went into the bathroom and looked in the mirror at my ugly, puffed face. "You're going to be held accountable," I told the face. I took the bottle of Scotch, sat in the back closet, and drank till I passed out. When I came to, it was after midnight. My apartment was pitch black and I didn't want any lights. As long as it was dark I might be dreaming. There was a little Scotch left in the bottle and I drank it down. Still with the lights out, I changed into my jeans and put on a black sweater and a black parka, put a small butcher knife in my pocket, and set out for Ted's place. I didn't know what I was going to do when I got there. I kept my hand on the knife in my pocket, very much afraid that I would be attacked. I looked up at Ted's windows. No lights, so I sat down on the porch to wait for him.

I got cold fast. Maybe this wasn't such a good idea. Maybe if I went back to my place, Ted would be there. I crept back home. No one was there and no one had been there. I drank the beer in the refrigerator and passed out again.

First thing the next morning, I threw on some clothes and drove over to Ted's. His landlord let me in and when I knocked on Ted's door there was no answer. I felt around the ledge where Ted always hid his key, found it, and let myself in. The bed was made—maybe he hadn't come home at all. I poked around the room looking for evidence and I found it. In his garbage can was a note from a girl named Marcy. "Saw you out riding your bicycle in the sun. Came by to visit but you weren't here. You missed out!" By the time Ted burst into the room I was lying on his bed, hysterical.

"What are you doing here?" he said, coming towards me. I sat up and started scooting backwards, away from him. I didn't want him to touch me.

"Are you all right?" I rolled off the bed and shot past him. He reached out and grabbed me and wrapped his arms around me. I was shaking with rage. I had so much to say that I was speechless. "Stay here until I get back," he told me. I nodded, but as soon as I heard him go out the front door I ran after him. He was just getting into a sporty red car. That must be her car. Maybe I should follow him. "Go back to my room and wait for me," he shouted as he drove off. I sat on his porch steps and put my head on my knees and rocked back and forth and moaned and moaned.

"*Gut Gott im Himmel. Was ist los?*" said his landlady.

"Just about everything," I told her and walked away.

I drove home and put the car in the garage. I was too tired to get out of the car. I heard footsteps running along the side of the garage. I thought I had cried myself out, but when I saw Ted's face the tears began again. I sprang out of the car so fast I think I scared him. I grabbed his shirt and began pushing and pulling at him. "I wish I was bigger than you. I'd beat the shit out of you!" I screamed.

He steered me into the house, out of earshot of the neighbors. I kept screaming at him. "When did you stop loving me? Did you ever really love me? Why didn't you tell me?" I went on and on, out of control. I ran to the bathroom and locked myself in.

Ted stood outside the bathroom door. "Please come out here and talk to me," he was saying.

"Get out of here and leave me alone. I hate you. I hate you. I hate you." The berserk sound of my own voice scared me. I was starting to feel detached from myself. I wondered what the people upstairs must be thinking.

"I'm going to get Angie," Ted shouted over my shouting. "Will that make you feel better?"

"Oh yes," I said sarcastically, "that will make everything fine. You get Angie and then things will be swell again."

Within a few minutes, Ted was back with Angie, who had a towel wrapped around her wet hair. He had crashed in on her while she was in the shower and scared the hell out of her.

"Why didn't you call me?" she said.

What good would that do? I wondered. Would that make Ted love me? What was the point? Angie and I talked. Ted said little. I wanted to know more about this other woman, Marcy. He told me she was just somebody he worked with at Harborview. How long had they been dating? Well, they had spent the Fourth of July together, he said.

"All day? You must really like her. Where did you go?" I felt like a kamikaze pilot.

"I don't think that is important. Telling you the details will only cause you more hurt." I knew why he didn't want to go on.

"You went rafting, didn't you? You went rafting with Marcy in the raft I gave you as a present." I only wished the raft was here so I could slice it into a million yellow ribbons.

At last I sent Ted away. I was tired. I spent the next few days with Angie: talking, drinking, crying, ranting, raving, crying some more. Ted looked in from time to time.

I finally realized that life was going to go on. I went on a shopping spree and bought myself a bunch of new clothes. One evening I was trying on a new nightgown in a nice store. I looked good in it and I wanted it, but then I thought, "What for?" I knew Ted would be back for sex. Over the years our sex life had been a strong bond between us, our desire rising and falling in cycles, but always tender and gratifying for me, and I knew why. I loved him with all my heart. He probably liked our sex because it was available, nothing more.

I bought the nightgown, admitting sadly to myself that if this was the only way I could be a part of Ted's life, I would settle for it.

About two weeks later Ted called for a date. Over steaks and beer, we made small talk. My job was fine. His job was fine. I had talked to Molly in Utah and she was fine. My parents were fine. Angie and I had been spending a lot of time together and, yes, Angie was fine, too.

Suddenly Ted grabbed my hand. "I'm sorry for what I've done," he blurted out. "I love you so much. Being with someone else was the loneliest experience of my life. I don't know why I jeopardized everything. Maybe, if you are willing—if you think you can forgive me, maybe we could start over. . . ."

I looked into those beautiful blue eyes, and I couldn't decide whether to slug him or flip out of my chair backwards and do handsprings across the room. Things were going to be okay. Things were going to get back to normal. But things were never really the same again.

Ted's job at Harborview ended and he threw himself into Governor Dan Evans's re-election campaign. He was working as a volunteer, but he had hopes of a paying position. Even if he didn't get paid, the experience and the contacts would be worth a million dollars. He was enthusiastic and busy. I decided to make some changes in my life and got a parttime job with an environmental agency. I did a little telephone work for McGovern's presidential campaign, and Ted thought that was awful, working for a Democrat. I was a poll watcher for McGovern on Election Day, and after the polls closed, Ted and I went to Evans's victory party. I didn't know a soul, so I stuck by Ted's side, feeling stupid, boring, and ugly. Eventually I slipped away to a tavern and drank until it was time to go. Ted couldn't understand why I got so tongue-tied around people.

Ted and I planned to go to the Governor's Inauguration Ball in January of 1973, so we went to Northgate Mall to buy a new dress. Molly and I liked a red number that Ted thought was too flashy. He picked out a black knit that was pretty in a conservative way, and I bought it. On the way back to the car, Ted suddenly shoved the dress box at me and took off running on the icy pavement. I didn't know what was happening until a woman with two little kids started screaming and pointing at a man almost a block away that Ted was chasing. When Ted came back with a security guard and the purse-snatcher, I was awed at how fast he had responded and at his bravery. He told me he had cornered the man in a dead-end alley, and at the last moment had realized that the man might be armed. Fortunately, he wasn't.

Ted was making good money at a job in the King County Budget Office, a job he got after working briefly for the Seattle Crime Commission on a study of white-collar crime. He decided to buy a car. I helped him by going through the ads, and soon he had a brown Volkswagen of his own.

In the spring of 1973, Ted was appointed Assistant Chairman of the Washington State Republican Central Committee. He loved the work and the people he worked with, particularly his boss, the State Chairman. It upset me very much that with such a great job, Ted still continued to steal. One day in a hardware store, he began gathering up tools and putting them in a tool chest. At first, I paid little attention, but he seemed so intent on what he was doing that I said, "You're not going to steal those, are you?"

"Of course not," he said. But several days later I saw the tool chest in his car. I had had enough confrontations, so I said nothing.

In the early summer I went sailing with a girlfriend and stumbled on a pocket of eligible men. One of them, Greg, needed someone to crew for him on his Hobie Cat, a sixteen-foot catamaran. There wasn't much to crewing, just shifting from one side of the boat to the other and sometimes going out in the trapeze, a sling affair that suspended a person over the water and kept the boat from turning over. It was great fun, and I made plans to crew for Greg again.

I liked the idea of making Ted jealous. Every time I tried to talk to him about our relationship it ended up the same way: I was insecure; I was too clingy. As far as he was concerned, our relationship was fine the way it was. When I asked him point blank whether he was dating anyone, he would look me straight in the eye and say no. When I told him about sailing with Greg, he told me I was taking a big chance, that I was probably going to ruin everything.

At the next regatta, I was helping Greg get the boat ready when I looked up and saw Ted on a bridge, watching me. I tried to talk to him, but he wouldn't answer, so I walked away, feeling his eyes drilling holes in my back. I wasn't going to let him spoil my good time.

Greg and I planned a bicycle and ferry trip to Victoria, British Columbia. I told Ted about it one morning as we were driving to work. He blew up and started driving like a madman. At the first chance, I got out of the car. I had walked about four blocks when Ted darted out of an alley in front of me. When he saw me, he jumped back. Then he was behind me, following me. Just as I got to work, he fell in step alongside me.

"You're making a big mistake, Elizabeth. I love you very much, and you're taking my love and destroying it."

"*I'm* destroying it!" I couldn't believe my ears. "You tell me you love me, but you don't act like it."

The evening Greg was to pick me up, Ted came over early and refused to leave. He had been drinking and his tears flowed freely. He wished I wouldn't go. I was steamed. I told him that I'd had enough, that I was sick of his words, words, words. If he wanted to stay and make a fool of himself, go ahead. He left. I went on my trip with Greg and we had a platonic good time.

When I returned I found a letter:

> *It's Friday evening. You're gone and I've never been so alone in my life. The memory of your face haunts me. The memory of our times together is so fine that the fact that I've lost you seems unreal. I'm perfectly stunned. Cigarette upon cigarette does nothing. You've left and I can think of nothing but that I love you. I love you now. I loved you in the past. I'll love you as long as I draw breath. . . . With tears in my eyes, I punish myself. Shaking my head, I can't believe I have driven you to find someone else. Your smile, your hand in mine, your loving daughter, the three of us together, these memories are the fondest memories I can ever hold. My insensitivity has destroyed everything. . . . I am looking inward as you told me to.*
>
> *I love you. I want you. Forever.*
>
> *Love,*
> *Ted*

There would be more such letters. And as often as I had told Ted that actions spoke louder than words, all he had to do was say the right ones. I told Greg that I couldn't see him anymore. Ted was attentive and loving for about a month; then we slipped into the familiar pit-stop routine.

In August my car was stolen and when I got it back, the only thing I could tell was missing was an Oriental knife that Ted had put in the glove compartment a couple of weeks earlier, saying that some friends had given it to him.

Three days later, Ted borrowed my car and, two blocks from my house, nearly totaled it. I had it fixed and drove it another fifty thousand miles.

In the fall, Ted started night law school at the University of Puget Sound in Tacoma. Now that he was a student again, I saw more of him. Occasionally he took me to class with him and I enjoyed that. I was trying to change so he would love me as he used to. My dependency bugged him, so I tried to get involved in things of my own.

I went skiing every Friday night. I liked to ski, but I loved the drinking that went along with it: hot buttered rums and coffee nudges. A couple of times, I never even put my skis on. Strange as it seemed, I started going to church again. I was feeling a lot of guilt about the kind of life I was living, and I prayed that I would learn something at church that would get my life back on track again.

Ted came skiing with me sometimes, but our favorite pastime was playing chess with Molly's toy chess set and drinking hot spiced wine. For Christmas I gave Ted a really nice hand-carved chess set. He had picked out a special present for me—a really nice hand-carved chess set.

As usual, Molly and I went home for Christmas. When my parents asked me about Ted, I didn't know what to tell them. I still thought we would get married when the time was right, but I had no idea when that time would be.

When we returned, Ted was wearing an expensive-looking red parka, a Christmas present from his mom, he said. He had on a Head brand ski sweater, another present from his mom. In his room there was a nice antique clock on the wall— from his mom. His mom was on a tight budget. I asked him if he had stolen anything lately. His indignation was so intense, I almost believed him.

— CHAPTER SEVEN —

Early in January 1974, a young woman was attacked as she slept in her house near the University District. She was raped and beaten unconscious. Her roommates were home, but they heard nothing, and she wasn't discovered until the next day.

I felt safe enough in the old house I lived in. There were four men renting the upstairs bedrooms and sharing a kitchen and bathroom. There were two more men living below me in the basement apartment. I felt confident that if anyone broke in, help was right at hand. I couldn't imagine a silent intruder, silently assaulting a woman, silently slipping away.

On January 31, Lynda Ann Healy, a University of Washington student, disappeared from her bedroom in the basement of a house a few blocks west of mine. She had stayed up late watching TV with her roommates, and had gone to bed as usual, but the next morning, when one of her roommates went into her room to look for her, she was gone. Her bed was neatly made, and her electric alarm clock sat buzzing on the bedside table. When the police inspected her room, they pulled the covers back and found blood on her pillow. They also found blood on her nightgown, which had been hung in the closet.

In February, a little girl who lived just south of the University District disappeared while she was playing in her front yard.

In June, a young woman named Georgann Hawkins disappeared without a trace as she walked from her boyfriend's fraternity house to her sorority house, three blocks south of my place.

Like most women living in the University District, I was deeply disturbed by these disappearances. Walking at night from my garage to my front door scared me. One day I was looking for something in the back seat of my car in the garage when a seedy-looking man stuck his head in the car and asked if he could borrow a screwdriver. I must have jumped a foot. I couldn't help thinking of those young women and how they had vanished without any clues.

Ted and I weren't getting along very well. In March, I had come home from a skiing weekend to find him in my apartment, upset and in tears. He said he had asked the landlord to let him in because he had to see me. He was doing badly in law school and had decided to drop out. I was surprised; I had no idea his schoolwork wasn't going well. He looked haggard, and when we sat on the couch, he put his head in my lap and cried. I stroked his hair and tried to get him to talk, but the words came haltingly. He couldn't concentrate, he said, but he didn't understand why. He felt that he was spinning his wheels. Being a lawyer meant everything to him, but he was terribly afraid that he wasn't going to make it.

I searched for things to say. I knew he would be a great lawyer if he could make it through law school. Maybe UPS was the wrong place. It was true, he said, that night school didn't feel like a "real" law school. Maybe a change of scene would help. The University of Utah had accepted him before; maybe he would reapply there.

Within weeks he had reapplied and was accepted for the coming fall. He would be moving to Salt Lake City. He talked about it a lot but said nothing about my going with him. I waited and waited for him to bring it up until I couldn't stand it any longer.

"Am I going or am I staying?" I asked him.

"It's up to you," he said. "You can come if you want."

I accused him of taking me for granted. He accused me of being insecure. The question of my moving to Utah was left dangling.

In June, Ted went to work for the State Department of Emergency Services in Olympia, and our time together shrank further. Olympia is a two-hour drive from Seattle. Some nights he stayed with a friend in Olympia. Some nights with his parents in Tacoma, some nights at his place in Seattle. We talked on the phone every day and he still came to my place a couple of times a week. Usually we'd go out to eat, and then he would go back to his place to sleep and I'd go back to my place to lie awake and think. I was hurt that he hardly ever wanted to make love. There had to be someone else. I wished I knew what she was like so I could be more like her.

The Fourth of July fell on a Thursday, so I had a four-day weekend. On Saturday, Ted and I piled into his VW with his rubber raft and my inner tubes in the back seat, and his bike tied to the ski rack, and headed east to go rafting on the Yakima River. It was a beautiful summer day and we were both in good spirits. Molly was with my parents for a month, and I was on my own.

We stashed the bike in some bushes by the river, then drove a few miles upstream and unloaded the raft. We would float down to the bike. Ted would ride the bike back to the car, tie it on, and then drive back down to pick up me and the raft. We had done this at least half a dozen times before.

The river was wide and slow, the water so cold it hurt. We scrambled in with our beer and suntan lotion and began to float downriver. The beer, the sun, and the water made all of life seem golden, at least for that day. Ted was quiet as we drifted slowly, daydreaming.

After a while we pulled up on a small island and had lunch, hardly talking, not wanting to disturb the perfect peace of the afternoon. Then we climbed back into the raft and pushed out into the river again.

About an hour later, I was sitting on the edge of the raft, paying attention to nothing in particular, when suddenly and without warning, Ted lunged at me, put his hands on my shoulders, and pushed me into the river. The plunge into the icy water took my breath away. I came up sputtering and grabbed the rope on the edge of the raft, too dazed for the moment to do more than hang on. I looked up at Ted and our eyes locked. His face had gone blank, as though he was not there at all. I had a sense that he wasn't seeing me. I struggled to pull myself into the raft. He didn't move, he didn't speak. I could find no expression on his face.

"Why do you have to ruin everything?" I began when I could finally talk. "That's not funny at all."

He still looked at me as if I were a stranger. Then he looked away and said, "It was no big deal. Can't you take a joke?"

On the way home we alternately bickered about what had happened and fell into long, unhappy silences. When we got to my house, he refused to unload the car. I grabbed what I needed, hurried up the steps, and slammed the front door behind me as he roared off.

The next day, Sunday, July 7, Ted came over in the afternoon with all the stuff still in the car. When I asked him where he'd been, he said he'd gone to Lake Sammamish, a few miles east of the city. I asked him what he had done there.

"Nothing," he said. "I walked along the water and thought, and then I ran into some friends. I just came over to unload the car." He was obviously still angry, but I wasn't about to apologize.

We talked every day on the phone during the week, as usual, and gradually the battle faded. We spent an evening together in the middle of the week, and it was as if nothing had happened.

The following Saturday, the thirteenth, the weather was still clear and hot. After cleaning the house and doing the laundry, I rode my bike to Green Lake to lie in the sun. The park was full of people, and when a Frisbee landed on me, I tossed it back to its owner. He was handsome and friendly, and I felt a stray tug. But he thanked me and moved on without inviting me to join the game. I was bored and lonely.

That night I called Ted at his parents' house to ask if he'd like to do something with me the next day.

"No, I can't. I have other things to do."

"What other things?"

"Just things, Liz."

I hung up feeling terrible.

The next morning, Sunday, July 14, as I was getting ready to leave for church, there was a knock on the door and Ted breezed in, full of morning good cheer, acting as if nothing was wrong between us. I was hurt and furious, but I didn't want to keep the battle going.

Ted wanted to know my plans for the day. I planned to go to church and then to a beach, but I hadn't decided which beach. He pressed me to tell him. *Maybe he'll join me later,* I thought, *to make up.*

"I guess I'll go to Carkeek Park," I said. We walked out of the house together, kissed coolly, and parted.

Carkeek Park was crowded that day, full of children and beer and handsome young men. I lay on the beach reading *All the President's Men*, turning restlessly. Hour after hour went by but Ted didn't show up. Late in the afternoon, a high, thin layer of clouds obscured the sun, and I went home.

I was stepping out of the shower when Ted phoned; I stood dripping on the floor as he asked me to have dinner with him. He was at the door in ten minutes, starving, he said.

The university student newspaper had just run a hamburger sweepstakes and declared the hamburgers at a bowling alley near Green Lake the best in town. Ted flopped in a chair while I got ready to go. He had a cold that seemed much worse than it had been that morning. He was so stuffed up he could hardly talk, and he looked tired. I asked him what he'd been doing. He just cleaned his car, he said, and helped his landlord with yardwork.

The hamburgers lived up to their reputation—good and big. It was all I could do to finish one of them, but Ted ate two and then wanted to go to Farrell's Ice Cream Parlour for dessert. I had hoped our dinner would give us a chance to talk about our fight, maybe even to settle how he felt about me, but when I began, I could see that he wasn't particularly interested.

"Yeah, I understand what you mean," he said, as though that took care of the matter.

I could see that he didn't feel well, so I stopped pushing. He was unusually quiet. As I looked at him across the table, I was struck by how close together his eyes looked. They were a little puffy from his cold, but it was odd that I had never noticed it before.

After dinner we went for ice cream, but we didn't linger. Ted wanted to go home and sleep; his cold was getting worse by the hour. But the ski rack we'd used the weekend before to carry his bicycle was still on his VW, and tired as he was, he decided to put it back on my car. It took about fifteen minutes in the fading twilight. It was dark when he finished and went home.

Ted stayed home ill on Monday. After work I took him some orange juice, a can of chicken soup, and my copy of *All the President's Men*.

On Wednesday the seventeenth, the morning paper reported that two young women had disappeared from Lake Sammamish State Park on Sunday. There had been a huge crowd at the lake that day—forty thousand people had turned out for a promotion staged by a beer company and a radio station. The two women, Denise Naslund and Janice Ott, had disappeared several hours apart, and it seemed possible that the same person might be responsible for both disappearances. The police were asking anyone with information about the two women to contact them. Within a few days, the papers reported that several witnesses had overheard Janice Ott talking to a man who had his arm in a sling. He was described as a smooth talker, possibly with a British accent, wearing expensive-looking tennis clothes. He had asked her to help put a sailboat on top of his car. She was last seen pushing her bicycle towards the parking lot chatting with the man who had introduced himself as "Ted." The car was described as a bronze or metallic-colored Volkswagen. Pictures of the women were in the papers. They were young and attractive, and both had long hair—just like the two women who had disappeared earlier from the University District.

In a phone call I told Ted what I'd read in the papers. He was back on his feet and at work. He wanted to know everything I had heard.

"They said he asked the first woman to help him put a sailboat on top of his VW," I said. "And that his name was Ted. I guess Ted's going to be a hot name for a while."

"Yeah. And I guess it's a good thing the guy didn't ask for help with a rubber raft," he joked.

We talked about other things: Ted was feeling good about his job, preparing a budget for the department. He'd never done a budget before and he was really learning a lot. His cold was better, but he was still tired.

For the next few days, reports of police interviews with witnesses from Lake Sammamish continued. Janice Ott's family offered a reward for the return of her bicycle. The radio was on in the office all day long because the Senate Watergate hearings were in progress, so I heard a lot of news. The newspapers were full of speculation, not only about the possible connection with the disappearances from the University District, but about reports that as many as seven young women had vanished from the Northwest since the beginning of the year. Donna Manson had disappeared from the campus of Evergreen State College in Olympia on March 12; Susan Rancourt had disappeared from Central Washington State College in Ellensburg, about a two-hour drive from Seattle, on April 17; Roberta Kathleen

Parks had disappeared from Oregon State University in Corvallis, 235 miles south of Seattle, on May 6. Later the police added the name of Brenda Ball to the list. She was last seen at 2:00 A.M. on June 1 at the Flame Tavern in south Seattle. The newspapers printed pictures of the women. They were all young and attractive, with long hair. The Seattle *Post-Intelligencer* published a police sketch of the "Ted" suspect. It didn't look like anyone I had ever seen.

It was spooky. When Angie and I wanted to lie out in the sun the next weekend, we decided to stay on the deck of her houseboat, rather than go to a beach. Ted came over to join us for a while, then went home to sleep off the last of his cold.

I was still stewing about Ted, fighting off the sinking feeling that he was moving out of my life. In the years we had been together he had become even more polished, even more sophisticated, moving through the world as though it belonged to him. I hadn't changed; I was going to be left behind. The thought of him in Utah going out with other women was unbearable.

On Monday afternoon, July 22, I had coffee with one of the men I worked with. As we were walking back through the long corridor from the hospital cafeteria, he pulled a newspaper clipping from his pocket and handed it to me. "Don't you think this looks like someone you know?"

The clipping was another police sketch, this one from the Seattle *Times*. I didn't read the *Times* regularly and hadn't seen this sketch before. Underneath the picture, my friend had underlined the name "Ted." "Doesn't your Ted have a VW?" he said in a joking way.

"But not metallic," I said. The drawing did look vaguely like Ted. I tried to laugh, but it stuck in my throat. I went back to my desk and stared at the clipping, then put it in the pocket of my backpack. I took it out several times to look at it, then put it back. I couldn't concentrate on my work. I watched the clock until it was time to go.

I rode my bike home in a hurry, went straight to my photo albums, and started pulling out pictures of Ted. The jawline was strikingly similar to the sketch. The little laugh lines under the eyes were the same, and there was a quality about Ted's eyes that I saw in the drawing. But there were discrepancies, too. The suspect had straight hair; Ted's was curly.

I took one of the photos and the sketch and headed for Angie's houseboat. I needed to talk. I stopped for a six-pack of beer, drove to the dock, and walked down the wooden planks. Angie let me in.

"What's wrong? You look awful."

"Angie, you've got to promise me that you'll never tell anyone about this. I think I'm going crazy." I shoved the newspaper clipping and the photo of Ted at her.

She looked from one to the other and then at me. "So?"

"I know I'm crazy, but I think they look a little alike. And then there's all the coincidences. It's all just weird."

"Okay," she said. "Stop saying you're crazy and weird and we'll talk. Where did you get this picture? What coincidences? When did you start thinking about this?"

I told her how I got the clipping and what it did to me. I listed the coincidences: "The accent. The witnesses said the suspect had a British accent. You remember the first night we met Ted in the bar, we thought he was from back East because of the way he talks? The suspect wore expensive-looking tennis clothes, and you know how Ted dresses in the best of everything."

"Just because he wears Adidas doesn't make him a murderer. Weren't you with him that Sunday?"

"In the evening. But I spent the day by myself. . . . I don't know. . . . It's just that the name, the Volkswagen, the cast, the expensive clothes."

"Cast? What does that have to do with Ted?" Angie asked me.

I took a long pull on my beer. It was beginning to take the edge off my anxiety. "Do you remember me telling you about the plaster of Paris?" She shook her head. "Well, once, a couple of years ago, I was going through Ted's desk drawers while he was taking a bath—you know how snoopy I am—and I found some plaster of Paris at the back of a drawer. I asked Ted about it and he said he didn't know why, but he had taken it when he was working at the medical supply house. He said a person never could tell when he was going to break a leg, and we both laughed. Now I keep thinking about the cast the guy at Lake Sammamish was wearing—what a perfect weapon it would make for clubbing someone over the head."

"Oh, please," Angie said, rolling her eyes. "You're forgetting a few things. The Volkswagen in the news is metallic bronze. Ted's is hardly metallic." That was true. The tan paint on his VW had weathered and looked sort of dull. "Besides," she went on, "if he was going to abduct someone, would he stroll up and introduce himself by his real name? Liz, you don't go with someone for four years and not know what they're about. You know Ted. You know his morals. Unless there's something you're not telling me about, then I don't know why this has you so upset."

"Well I have been thinking about his morals—you know the way he steals things? I always made excuses for him, but when he continued to rip things off even after he got those good jobs, well I started to think there might be something more to it, like maybe he enjoys getting away with the con."

"You're right," she said, "the stealing is stupid, but there is a big difference between stealing something and murdering someone."

"But I've been thinking about it. Somewhere there is someone who knows what happened to the two women who disappeared that day and to the two women who disappeared from my neighborhood. This is a real person. He isn't suspected, so he can move around freely."

I struggled to maintain control. "It's not so much the name or the car or the cast. . . . It's this dreadful feeling I can't shake. I know it can't be true, but it hit me like a ton of bricks when I saw the picture. I can't figure it out. I can't think. I feel like my head's on backwards. Angie, you've got to help me!" I grabbed her arm so hard that it scared her.

"Let me think," she said. "Have you prayed about this?"

I nodded. "It didn't do any good."

"Give me a minute. I can't think either." She sat quietly and I thought she was praying, so I looked out the window at the blue sky and the colorful houseboats. It was too nice a day for this, I thought.

"It seems to me," Angie started slowly, "that you should call the police."

I was shocked. I couldn't believe what she had said. "Can you imagine what Ted would do when he found out?"

"I mean call them anonymously. I'm sure you're wrong, but how else are you going to get rid of that feeling? How long are you willing to feel the way you do?" We began thinking of questions to ask the police.

Our first question was whether the VW was positively metallic in color. That could rule out Ted right away. Then we decided to ask if "their" Ted had a cold, and if he wore a watch on his right wrist. "My" Ted was left-handed and always wore his watch on his right wrist.

We wouldn't call from Angie's: There was a chance the police would be tracing all the calls that came in about the case. We got in my car and drove to a phone booth in a supermarket parking lot near Green Lake. We knew that the police had set up a "Ted Hotline," but how were we going to get the number? Call Information?

"Hello, Information? I want the number I call to find out if my boyfriend is a murderer." We sat in the car looking at the empty phone booth. I found a dime. Angie had to get up her nerve to get out of the car. She had to practice what she was going to say. She had never called the police in her life, not about anything.

I sat in the car while she phoned. For me it was like being on hold. I don't know if it was a long time or a short time, but she was back in the car and I was asking her questions as fast as I could.

"What did they say? What did you say? Did they ask your name?"

"He told me all reports about the VW were that it was metallic. No reports mentioned a cold," she said.

"What about the watch?"

She'd been so rattled she'd forgotten to ask about the watch. I told her to go back and call again.

"No way!" she said. "They'll know it's me. You do it. It's easy. They don't want to know who you are or who you're calling about."

She was right. I had to do it myself, and it was as easy as she said. I got the number again from Information. I asked the policeman if the suspect had a watch on his right arm. He said that none of the witnesses had mentioned anything about a watch.

We had done it. I drove out of the parking lot without any idea of where I was going. After a few blocks I pulled over and parked. I opened another beer. We had called the police, but I didn't feel relieved and it wasn't over.

Suddenly Angie looked at me and laughed. "Do you realize what you're doing?" she asked. "You're sitting in front of the Mormon Church, drinking a beer." I laughed, too. I needed some comic relief. With my luck the bishop would stroll by.

We went to the university library to read all the newspaper stories and learn everything we could about the disappearances. We paged through all the papers for the last week. One story described "Ted" as five-foot-six or five-foot-seven—several inches shorter than my Ted.

The VW was described as metallic gold—Ted's was dull brown—and there was no mention of a ski rack on the back. There was a different composite drawing, too. It gave the suspect curly hair, but the resemblances to my Ted weren't there.

The discrepancies were reassuring. "It sounded like Ted," I said, "all that stuff about the expensive tennis clothes, the white Adidas, and the way he talks, and the business about asking for help with his sailboat. Ted is always talking about when he'll own a sailboat. But this doesn't look like him at all."

I drove Angie home, wondering what had gotten into me. Then I drove to Ted's place. I wanted to see him, to see that he was the same Ted I knew. I was relieved to find him home, and he seemed glad to see me and the cold beer I brought on this hot summer night.

I lay on the floor in his room. We drank beer and talked aimlessly about ordinary things. I found my eyes traveling over every detail of his room, as if I was seeing everything for the first time. I noticed a pair of crutches in the corner by the door. Ted said they belonged to his landlord, and that he had offered to return them to the rental agency. There was a big knife—like a meat cleaver—on his desk. Ted showed me how the knife was specially designed to rock back and forth on its blade for dicing and mincing vegetables.

I went home and Ted joined me later. He seldom spent the whole night anymore, but that night we fell asleep next to each other after making love.

— CHAPTER EIGHT —

I don't remember how many times I went over every detail I could think of about Sunday, July 14, the day the two young women disappeared from Lake Sammamish. There were stories in the papers almost every day. The police were searching the area around the lake with infrared cameras that were supposed to be able to detect newly disturbed earth, but they didn't find anything. There was some confusion about what time Janice Ott, the first of the young women, disappeared. The stories about Denise Naslund's disappearance agreed on four o'clock. It had been five or five-thirty when Ted called to ask me to have dinner with him that Sunday. I couldn't understand why Ted had gone to Lake Sammamish on July 7. We had never been there together and as far as I knew, Ted had never been there before.

I conspired with Angie to take Ted to her houseboat so she could see if he still looked normal to her. We arrived after dinner, and Ted talked and joked while he ate her leftover eggplant Parmesan. Angie and I agreed the next day: Nobody looked more normal than my Ted in her kitchen, talking and eating.

I talked to Ted on the phone every day. He was feeling pressured about the budget he was working on and about his move to Utah. I was leaving in a few days to spend a week with my family and bring Molly back; Ted asked me to find him an apartment in Salt Lake City.

I did as he asked, but it seemed to me that I was doing the work of getting him set for law school without anything in it for me. I spent hours in Salt Lake City poring over the rental ads and traipsing up and down stairs of places with pink flamingos on the wallpaper.

Finally I found an apartment I knew Ted would like in an old house in a neighborhood called The Avenues, near the University of Utah. The house was being remodeled, but it would be ready by fall. I called Ted to tell him about it, and he was pleased. He would meet Molly and me at the airport.

We caught an early flight and landed in Seattle about nine on a Sunday morning. When we walked off the plane, Ted was nowhere in sight.

We headed for the subway train that takes people to the main terminal and baggage area. A train pulled up, the doors opened, and there he stood. I felt as if I'd been hit in the stomach. All his curly hair was gone. It was the shortest haircut I'd ever seen on him, and it changed his appearance drastically. I went through the motions of greeting and kissing him as though in a dream.

Molly thought the new haircut looked funny and she told him so. "Why did you do it?" she asked.

"Because I just decided to," he said.

Molly chattered all the way home from the airport. She wanted to get home and go out and play, to go swimming right away. We decided to go to Green Lake for the afternoon.

We loaded Ted's car with the raft, two inner tubes, and all our picnic stuff. We stopped on the way to the lake to get some beer. It was illegal to drink in the park, but we'd be careful. It was the kind of hot, sunny day that makes cold beer taste great. Our picnic ended badly. I watched from the shore as Ted rowed the raft with Molly swimming along behind. He stayed so far ahead of her that she got tired and frightened. When they got to shore she was in tears and I was furious.

"Why do you have to push her so hard? Nobody thinks it's funny but you!"

"Oh, Liz, not again. Will you stop! Just because you baby her doesn't mean everyone else should, too."

We gathered up our things and headed for his car. As we were loading it, I reached under the front seat to retrieve Molly's stray sock and my fingers touched a hatchet. My blood stopped flowing. I pulled myself together enough to ask, casually, "What's this for, Ted?"

"I chopped down a tree at my parents' cabin last week."

I was so rattled, I left the oars on the ground next to the car and we didn't notice that they were missing until we got home. Ted was really annoyed with me. He was sure there was no point in going back for them, that they would be stolen. We argued, but we went back, and they were there where I'd left them.

When we got home again, I was so drunk I started to cry and couldn't stop. Ted wanted to know what I was crying about and I told him it was because he was moving away.

"You're crying because you drank too much," he said. "Everything will work out for us. You could have come with me if you'd wanted to."

I didn't argue with him. It had been a horrible day. I had felt safe in Utah with my family, but as soon as I got off the plane in Seattle I was hit with it again. I was now scared—not that Ted would hurt me or Molly, because that was inconceivable—but that he would find out what I was thinking.

I thought back over the years with Ted, trying to find what I might have overlooked before. He was not a violent person. When we argued he was always calm and reasonable; I was the one who lost control and yelled. I could count on the fingers of one hand the times that Ted had lost his temper since I'd known him. One of the times was the afternoon Molly and I had stopped by his room and found he had redecorated with a new television, a new stereo, a new typewriter, and several other things I knew he didn't have the money to buy. "You're nothing but a thief!" I had blurted out.

He grabbed my arm. "If you ever tell anyone about this, I'll break your fucking neck."

Later that night he came to my place crying, saying he didn't understand himself or why he took those things. He had given me a beautiful cutting board the previous Christmas. Had he stolen that? Had he stolen the presents he had given Molly? He confessed he had. I tried to explain to him that I would rather have no present than a stolen present. It wasn't so much the morality of it: I was afraid that he'd be arrested for shoplifting. He had sworn up and down that he wouldn't steal any more, but what stood out in my mind now, looking back, was his threat to break my fucking neck.

I spent a lot of time trying to figure out why I would even be thinking these terrible thoughts. Was I going crazy? Was it jealousy? Why did I try to keep building the case against Ted? I tried praying, but it didn't help. The only thing that did help was being with Ted. He was so normal, so absorbed in what he was doing and planning. He was looking for an old truck to move his things, and he was making lists of things for the move. He was collecting pots and pans for his new kitchen and was excited about having a whole apartment to himself, not just a room. And I was still wondering what would become of the two of us.

One night we finally talked about our future and assured each other that we'd stay together. But even then, I suspected that we were saying these things to each other because neither of us was willing to face the truth: that Ted was bored with me; that I was socially inadequate for the political circles he traveled in; that he would soon be looking for someone new. Still, I didn't give up hope altogether. Maybe this was only a bad time. Maybe we would pull through it somehow. There was no way of knowing. But just when I began to believe that there was nothing wrong anywhere except inside my head, something would happen to trigger my fears again.

The newspapers, radio, and TV news were filled with speculation and stories, pictures and rumors about the "Ted" case. There was no way to escape it.

For my morning coffee break on August 8, I took my cup of coffee and the morning paper out into the sun. What I read chilled me. The story was headlined *UW Coed's Encounter with a Man Like "Ted."* A young, female student had been walking in front of the Beta Theta Pi fraternity house about 12:30 A.M. on June 11, the night Georgann Hawkins had disappeared from the University District, when she encountered a man on crutches carrying a briefcase. He was having a lot of trouble and was dropping the briefcase every few steps. The student helped him carry the case as far as her boyfriend's fraternity house and told him she would be out in a few minutes and could help him to his car if he needed it. She stayed over an hour, and when she came out, he was gone. Georgann Hawkins had last been seen about 1:00 A.M.

I had seen crutches in Ted's room. I dragged myself back to my office, terrified. I had to call Angie, but I could barely talk. I told her about the crutches and about the story in the paper.

"There's only one thing you can do," she said. "You'd better call the police." I knew she was right.

I went out to a pay phone and looked up the number of the Seattle Police Department's homicide unit. I was trying not to cry. I asked to speak with someone who was familiar with the "Ted" case, and when the officer who answered said that he was, I poured out one long scary sentence about being worried about my boyfriend, that he might be involved, that he sort of matched the descriptions, and that I had seen crutches in his room.

"What's your boyfriend's name?" the officer asked.

"I can't tell you," I answered. "I'm not sure he's involved, I'm just worried. Some things fit and some things don't."

"I can't talk to you over the phone," the officer said. "You need to come in and fill out a report. We're too busy to talk to girlfriends over the phone. How do you think we can . . ."

I hung up on him. I sat in the phone booth and prayed. "I don't know what you want me to do, God. Please help me."

I went back to watching and waiting, spending my days thinking, trying to find some end to the thoughts in my head, spending my nights drinking to shut down my mind.

One night in August, Ted called from his parents' house in Tacoma. He was crying, and his words came out slowly. He told me that he'd been driving near a shopping center in Tacoma and had seen the police chase a man down the street. "He was like an animal," Ted said. "He ran and ran with the police chasing him in their car, and when they caught him, he urinated all over himself." I wondered what he was trying to tell me, but when I tried to get him to tell me more about it, he changed the subject and started talking about the budget he was working on. I had to take what he told me at face value: Nothing else made sense. I was almost sure that I'd lost control of my thinking, that there was something seriously wrong with my mind, or that it was all part of the pain of Ted's leaving me. Finally, I began to look forward to his departure, hoping that once he was gone, all these weird thoughts would depart, too.

I still spent time with Ted. We were doing all our favorite things one last time. We went to our favorite tavern, the Deluxe, which was famous for its bargain steak dinners. We went to visit his parents together, and I wondered if it was the last time I would see them.

One day Ted took my car to Olympia because his was out of gas. He gave me his Chevron credit card and asked me to fill his car up when I got the time. While the service station attendant was filling the tank, I noticed a thick bunch of gas receipts over the visor. Feeling like a burglar, I pulled them down and went through them one by one. They were all from the area, and with shaking hands I put them back where I had found them. I decided to search his room.

The next afternoon I called Ted at his office in Olympia to make sure he was there and went straight to his room. Sometimes he left his room unlocked; sometimes he locked it and left the key on the doorframe. This time it was locked, and I couldn't find the key. I had to ask his landlord to let me in. I told him I was there to help Ted pack, but I beamed a silent message to him: "Don't tell Ted I was here."

There were cardboard boxes, already packed, on the floor. I started digging into them. I found more gas receipts and went through them: nothing out of the ordinary. I found a film cannister that was heavily taped with electrician's tape. I was tempted to take it but didn't dare. He might notice that it was gone. I found an eyeglass case full of every kind of key I could imagine. Did he break into houses with them? That was different from shoplifting. I found his cancelled checks. I pawed through a couple of months, not knowing what I was looking for, getting as frightened as if Ted might burst in on me at any moment. When I couldn't stand it any longer, I grabbed an envelope full of cancelled checks for the month of May 1974 and fled. Later that night, at home, I went through them. There were two that got my attention: one to a rental outfit, the other to a surplus store. The next day I called the rental company and told them I was balancing my checkbook and had a check that I couldn't identify. Could they tell me what it was for? The man said they didn't keep records for that kind of thing.

Angie was worried about where this obsession was taking me, so I tried not to talk to her about it as much.

Ted was working right down to the wire on his budget. The

Sunday before he was to leave, Molly and I went down to Olympia with him for the day. We took my TV set and parked Molly in front of it in a back room, and then I sat at a typewriter while Ted paced up and down behind me, dictating. It was a long day; Ted was way behind in the work and his deadline was Monday.

This was the Ted only I knew, I thought. Everyone else thought he was so well organized, but I had spent years helping him out of last-minute jams like this. He had always waited until the last possible moment to write papers and then showed up at my office and asked me to drop everything and type them. He took incompletes in many of his classes and had to make the work up later. Today was typical. It was midnight when we finished, and Ted left his budget on his boss's desk, tied with a big red ribbon.

Angie cooked a going-away breakfast for Ted on her houseboat. It was Labor Day weekend, still sunny and hot, and Ted took a last look at the lake and the matching blue sky above it. He would miss Seattle, he said, but he was glad to be starting fresh in Utah and convinced that he would finally be able to concentrate on getting his law degree. He tickled Molly one last time, gave Angie a hug, and then turned to me. We held each other for a long time, then kissed goodbye. Ted waved and honked as he drove off, his Boston fern beside him in the front seat.

CHAPTER NINE

Ted called me from Nampa, Idaho, to tell me he loved me. We had picnicked there on one of our trips to Utah. He called me again from outside of Salt Lake City to tell me where he was, and he called me from his apartment to tell me how much he loved the place I had found for him. We talked several hours a week, running up huge phone bills.

In mid-September 1974, the bodies of the two young women who had disappeared from Lake Sammamish were found in woods not far from the lake. According to the newspaper accounts, there were no clues and the police were still baffled. I told Ted about it, listening for some sort of reaction, but hearing none. The next time we talked he asked me if any more bodies had been found. His bringing it up like that scared the hell out of me.

In late October, I picked Angie up at the airport as she was returning from a trip to Utah. She seemed upset, but she waited until we were alone in the car to tell me what was wrong.

"I don't want to scare you," she said, "but it's happening in Utah right now."

I stared at her. I knew exactly what she meant.

"When my mom was driving me to the airport," she said, "I heard it on the radio. Deer hunters found the body of the daughter of the Midvale police chief. She'd been missing—just like the girls up here."

Tomorrow morning, I would have to call the police. I had fixed a nice dinner for Angie, but neither of us could eat. I drank the bottle of wine I'd bought and was awake most of the night. I visualized Ted and me married: He would be campaigning to be governor when it was revealed that his devoted wife had gone to the police in 1974, claiming that he was a murderer.

The next morning, I waited until everyone else in my department had gone on a break, and then I called the King County Police.

"Major crimes, Hergesheimer."

"I'd like to talk to someone who knows about the missing women cases." I was shaking and my voice was high and strained.

"I can help you," he said.

Even though I had rehearsed this a hundred times during the night, I didn't know how to begin. "I'm scared that a friend of mine is involved. I know I'm wrong, but there are some coincidences. My friend moved away and the crimes stopped, and now where he lives the same kind of thing is happening. Most of the time I think I'm crazy, but then I get scared that I'm right." I wanted to be businesslike and concise, but here I was rattled, talking about being crazy.

"Let's start at the beginning. What's your friend's name?"

I paused. I'd been at this point before. "I really don't want to say. I know you can't do much without his name, but it's just that I'm probably wrong. . . ."

"I understand. It makes my job harder but not impossible. What are the coincidences that you are worried about?"

He understood. I told him about the experience I'd had when I called the Seattle Police. "My friend drives a Volkswagen, but it's not metallic; sometimes he speaks in a formal way that could be mistaken for an accent; and his first name is Ted."

The detective's reaction was milder than I had expected. He wanted to know why I had called the Seattle Police. I told him about seeing the crutches in my friend's room. He wanted to know what was significant about that. I was amazed. Didn't he know that a man on crutches had been connected with the Georgann Hawkins case?

"Then you've been worried for a long time," he said.

"Oh yes! It's been so awful! I know I'm wrong, but I can't stop thinking about it." He pressed me for more. Why was I calling him today? I told him what Angie had heard on the radio and that my friend had moved to Salt Lake City in September.

"What is your relationship with your friend?" he asked.

"Well, we've gone together for five years," I said. I was getting worried about people coming back to the office. I told him I couldn't talk much longer.

"What's the next step?" he wanted to know. "I think, in order to put your fears to rest, we need to pursue this further."

"Could you call Salt Lake City and find out what is going on there? Maybe it isn't similar at all. Maybe they have made an arrest already."

"I'll do that. What's your phone number and I'll call you back."

"No, I'll call *you* back," I said. I was getting panicky.

"Well, what's your name? I need to know who is calling me back. I want to tell you that you're not the first girlfriend who has called about her boyfriend. They all felt about as bad as you do, but after we checked the guys out, the women were tremendously relieved."

I told him my name was Liz.

"Okay, Liz, you are for sure going to call me back, right? It is important that you call back. Give me an hour. My name is Randy Hergesheimer. Promise me that you'll call back in an hour."

Feeling like I was six years old, I solemnly promised to call him back in an hour. I just had time to call Angie before people drifted back to the office. She was leaving in a few days for Europe.

I called Hergesheimer back in two hours.

"I thought you had changed your mind," he said.

"I got real busy here," I lied. I had watched every move of the minute hand on the clock for the last two hours.

"Well, I called Salt Lake City," he said, and told me only what Angie had heard on the radio, about the body being found. "Let's talk about your friend some more," he said. I said I would call him back at lunchtime.

I went looking for the most out-of-the-way pay phone I could find. It was by itself on the mezzanine outside a large auditorium. I called Hergesheimer back.

He told me that right after the Lake Sammamish disappearances the police had done a massive study of VW owners named Ted. "There are more of them than you might think," he said. "What else made you worry about your friend?"

I told him about Ted going to Lake Sammamish the weekend of July 7.

"I go there a lot myself," he said.

"I've never been there," I answered, "and I don't think Ted had gone there before, either."

"But that wasn't enough to make you worry, was it? Is your boyfriend violent? What really started you going on this thing?"

I told him about the composite picture and my first anonymous call to the "Ted Hotline." It was hard for me to put the bits and pieces together in any way that would sound sensible. I said that two of the earlier disappearances had happened in my own neighborhood, in the University District.

"Where did your boyfriend live?" When I told him it was the U District, he quickly asked me if my friend's name—Ted—was short for Edward.

"No, it's short for Theodore," I said.

"You don't mean . . ." I could hear him shuffling papers, "Theodore R. Bundy?"

I was stunned. "How did you know that?"

"We checked him out last summer when his name was called in to the task force."

"By who?"

"A university professor."

So, Ted had already been checked out. I was at once relieved that I'd been worrying for nothing and indignant that anyone else would suspect my Ted of these horrible crimes.

"I still think we should get together," Hergesheimer said. "Would you come down here to talk to me?"

"No." I was emphatic.

"Would you meet me somewhere in the U District, say Herfy's?" he went on, naming a popular hamburger place. I hesitated. "You sound like you have been pretty upset by your worries. Discussing them with me can put an end to them once and for all."

I agreed to meet him in the Herfy's parking lot. After I hung up, I went into the ladies' room. The mirror confirmed what I felt: the worst case of blotches I had ever had.

We had gone through a long thing on the phone about how we would recognize each other, but I spotted him immediately that evening because he looked exactly like a detective sitting in a detective's unmarked car, waiting for someone. He had a stack of papers on the seat with an enlargement of Ted's driver's license photo on top.

We sat in Hergesheimer's car, and I asked him about the police checking Ted out earlier. I felt somehow tricked. He picked up Ted's picture and said, "This is proof. I couldn't have got it since you called this morning. We got it last summer."

We went back over everything: height, weight, hair color; the accent, the VW, the expensive-looking tennis clothes; whether Ted had a sailboat. I told him I had been with Ted the morning and the evening of July 14. He told me that when they checked Ted out, they found he had never been in trouble with the law and seemed to be clean in every way.

I hesitated, and then I began. "That's just it. There is a side to Ted that only I know. You see, he steals!" Hergesheimer kept looking at me as if I hadn't finished my sentence. "I mean he gets all dressed up in his fine clothes and then he shoplifts. He's taken everything from textbooks to a TV." I felt stupid. Hergesheimer was trying to catch a murderer, not a thief.

I went on. "Sometimes I think that Ted enjoys the 'con' of stealing things more than the stuff he stole. One of the few times I've ever seen him lose his temper was when I dropped over to his room and he had a new TV and a new stereo and a bunch of stuff I knew he couldn't afford. I was shocked and I told him he was nothing but a thief. He told me that if I ever told anyone, he would break my fucking neck."

"Does he have a violent temper? Did he put his hands on you when he threatened you? Did he ever hit you?"

I was embarrassed, but I told Hergesheimer about the only time Ted had hit me. It was early in our relationship and I was drunk. I couldn't remember what we were arguing about, but I kept telling Ted to "Go ahead and hit me. Go ahead!" Finally, he had slapped me. Ironically, it had happened in this very same Herfy's parking lot.

Hergesheimer asked me if there was anything in Ted's background that would affect the way he felt about women. I told him that Ted was illegitimate, and that he had been upset because his mom had never discussed it with him, but that he was still close to his mom and his brothers and sisters.

Then, looking straight into my eyes, Hergesheimer said, "What about your sex life?"

"Oh, we've had our ups and downs, so to speak." I was trying to cover my nervousness by being funny, but my face was beginning to flush. "We've had a pretty good sex life up until last summer, I guess. Then Ted just lost all interest in sex . . . he was under a lot of pressure with his job . . . and moving and all . . . maybe he had another girlfriend . . . I don't know."

"I know this is hard for you, but it is important," he said. How often? What positions? When? Where?

I didn't even talk about these things with Angie, but I told myself that this guy was a police officer. He'd heard it all before.

I told him that in the fall of 1973, Ted had brought a copy of a book called *The Joy of Sex* to my house. We had lain in bed and read through it. Ted sheepishly asked me if we could try bondage. I said sure, never dreaming that a year later I'd be sitting in a car telling a stranger about it. We'd had sex that way maybe three times, but I didn't like it, so we stopped. I tried to convince Hergesheimer that there was nothing unnatural about the way we made love.

Had Ted ever had any homosexual experiences that I knew about?

None. But during the past year he had talked about anal sex enough to make me wonder. Had we had anal sex? No, never. I couldn't think of anything less appealing.

Hergesheimer pulled out a piece of paper and asked me to look at it. It was a psychological profile, a list of characteristics that a psychiatrist thought the killer would possess. I read down the list: Ted didn't come even remotely close to fitting it. When I came to the line that said the killer probably hated animals and had a history of cruelty to them, I thought about all the strays Ted had brought to my house, the hamsters and guinea pigs and kittens he had given Molly.

Hergesheimer told me flatly that Ted didn't look like a suspect. He told me about a man he had investigated recently. Everything about him fit what the police were looking for and they spent a lot of time checking the guy out. When they picked him up it turned out he had an airtight alibi: He was on a fishing boat off Alaska on the day of the disappearances from Lake Sammamish. Hergesheimer's frustration was apparent in his voice. He talked about how much pressure there had been to solve the case, pressure from the public and pressure from his superiors. I really wished I could somehow help him.

He asked me if I would give him some recent pictures of Ted so, as a final check, he could show them to the witnesses from Lake Sammamish. I hesitated. Pictures would be concrete proof that I had called the police. I thought of my waking dream the night before, about Ted's campaign for governor. I tried to explain how I felt about giving him the pictures. He seemed to be getting annoyed with my ambivalence. It was getting late; he probably wanted to get home. I told him yes, he could have the pictures.

As he started his car, he turned to me and said, "Now you've told me absolutely everything that's been bothering you, right?" I bit my lip. I didn't know if I should bring up one last thing. He persuaded me that giving him "almost" all the information I had would clear up "almost" all my questions. If I wanted to be totally done with this, I would have to be a hundred percent honest with him. So I told him about the plaster of Paris I had found in Ted's desk drawer several years ago, and Ted's comment that you can never tell when you'll break your leg.

We drove the six blocks from Herfy's to my place in silence. It was past Molly's bedtime, but she was still up with the babysitter. I introduced the detective as my "friend" and tucked Molly in, then walked the babysitter home, to the end of the block. Neither of us liked walking down the dark street, but tonight, knowing there was a policeman in my living room, I felt safe.

When I got back, we started flipping through photo albums. He told me he thought Molly was a real cute kid and asked me how she got along with Ted. I told him how lucky I felt that she and Ted cared so much for each other. The albums were proof: a three-year-old riding on his shoulders; a five-year-old held up on her new bike; an eight-year-old held upside down by him. I wanted to tell Hergesheimer about all the trips, the dinners, everything we had shared, but I knew he didn't care. He picked up three snapshots and then pulled out a report form. His manner was businesslike.

"Spell your name. Give me your address. How old are you?"

I was tired. It seemed to take him forever to write down the things we'd talked about at Herfy's. At last he was ready to go. "I'll let you know what the witnesses say as soon as I show them the pictures," he said on his way out the door.

I called Angie and we talked into the night. I felt guilty and I felt relieved. She was leaving the next day for Europe and was upset about leaving me with so many worries, but she gave me an address in Paris—as if she could do anything from halfway around the world.

A week later my parents came for a visit. I tried to dazzle them with how well I was doing. I chattered about becoming involved with the University District Community Council and getting chosen for the board right away. I had accepted a church job that was keeping me busy. I rambled on about the night class I was taking. What I didn't tell them was that I had lost control of my mind and couldn't sleep at night unless I was drunk.

Ted called several times that week. It was easy for me not to think about having gone to the police when I was talking with him. He was just Ted, nothing else. It was after I hung up that I was consumed by guilt and hoped to God he never found out!

I had expected to hear from Hergesheimer right away. When almost a week had gone by with no word, I called him again from the same pay phone on the mezzanine.

"Hi, this is Liz. Have you shown those pictures to the Lake Sammamish witnesses yet?"

"What pictures?" he asked.

"Those pictures of Ted Bundy."

"Who is this again?" he asked, sounding irritated.

"This is Liz Kendall. I talked to you last week in the Herfy's parking lot." I had told this man the most intimate details of my life and he couldn't remember who I was. "I gave you three snapshots and you were going to show them to the witnesses from Lake Sammamish and call me back."

"Oh, yeah. I haven't had a chance to show them to the most reliable witness. I haven't been able to get ahold of her. Like I told you, I'll call you when I do."

More days went by without a word from Hergesheimer. I decided to call him again. In my imagination I could hear him say things like, "Don't call here any more." Or, "You're the one who ought to be locked up, lady. You're the one with the problem."

As it turned out, Hergesheimer was on vacation.

One day I called a woman I barely knew and asked her if she would join me at the afternoon break. I was so lonely. As we got our coffee, she suggested we join her boyfriend and his friends from the Prosthetics and Orthotics lab in the hospital. On the way back to our offices she said to me, "You noticed that good-looking guy named Jim? The reason I didn't use his last name when I introduced you is that he's Jim Ott. His wife, Jan, was murdered out by Lake Sammamish."

A terrible chill swept over me. I knew who had murdered his wife. Oh my God, was I responsible? I had done the only thing I knew to do. I had gone to the police. It was out of my hands now.

Weeks later I remembered that my ski rack was on Ted's car on July 14. Was that what happened to Janice Ott's bicycle?

Finally, Hergesheimer called me. He had shown the pictures to his best witness. He explained to me that a stack of photos is given to the witness and that she goes through them one by one. When she came to one of Ted, she pulled it out of the stack and balanced it on her knee. When she was finished, she took Ted's picture and put it back in the stack. The man was too old, she explained.

"That's hardly a positive I.D." Hergesheimer said.

"What does that mean?"

"I don't know what it means to you," he said, "but to me it means I'm going to put Ted Bundy in my done-it-twice file and file him away."

— CHAPTER TEN —

Around Thanksgiving, a young housewife named Vonnie Stuth vanished from her home in the south end of Seattle. My first reaction was relief—Ted was in Salt Lake City—but almost immediately, the police announced that they had a suspect and that the Stuth case was not related to the "Ted" murders.

I was trying to get on with my life as best I could, but it was hard. For my night class I was supposed to write a term paper based on research done in newspapers. As I headed for the newspaper reading room in the downtown public library, I knew that I would read the Salt Lake *Tribune* while I was there. Maybe the crime in Salt Lake had been solved.

As I browsed through the *Tribune,* I found myself reading about the Utah political scene and how the college football teams were doing. Then I came to the first article about the discovery of the body of Melissa Smith, the killing Angie had told me about. The article said that Smith, the daughter of Midvale's police chief, had been missing since the evening of October 18. That was the day before my dad's birthday, and my dad had spent his birthday deer hunting with Ted, Ted had called me several times on the eighteenth; he had never been hunting before, and he was excited about it.

I started going through papers more rapidly, looking for more details. I was stunned by what I found next. On November 8, a young woman had been abducted from a shopping mall by a man posing as a police officer. The woman had escaped from the man's *Volkswagen* as he tried to handcuff her. The man had struggled with the woman, had managed to get the handcuffs on one wrist, and had tried to hit her with a crowbar, but she managed to get away. Later that night, a young woman named Debbie Kent disappeared from a high school parking lot in Bountiful, Utah, thirty miles north of the attack on the first young woman. The police had found a key in the high school lot that fit the handcuffs attached to the first woman's wrist.

Get up, I told myself. *Get up and go see your bishop.*

By the time I got to the church, I was detached from the horror I had felt at the library, but when I entered the bishop's office and shook his hand, I came unglued. I had been trying for so long to maintain a calm and poised façade, to at least look normal from the outside. Now I sat in front of my bishop sobbing and wringing my hands. He listened patiently, trying to make sense out of my story as I jumped back and forth. I kept telling him that I thought I was persecuting Ted and I didn't know why.

In a calming voice, my bishop began talking to me about decisions. He told me that he sometimes agonized over simple ones, and had learned that the only way to get peace of mind was to make a decision, take it to the Lord, and if it was a right decision, I would feel a confirmation in my heart. I explained to him how intensely I had prayed to know what was right and what I should do.

"God gave you free agency. You have to exercise it accordingly," he told me.

"That's just it," I told him. "I *am* trying to do what's right. I thought I had to go to the police, but when they told me I was wrong I was *still* scared. At the library, I felt like claws were tearing my soul to shreds."

"I think the police should be made aware of what you read in the papers," he said. "Give them the burden. They will know whether it bears pursuing."

"I can't call them again. They've already checked Ted out twice. They think I'm a hysterical nut out to get my boyfriend."

"Do you want me to call them?" he asked.

Relief swept over me. I gave him Hergesheimer's number and went home to start my nightly ritual of drinking myself to sleep. I knew the bishop would be disappointed if he could see me, but what else could I do? While I was having my first drink, I got out a calendar and looked at the date of the attempted abduction by the man in the Volkswagen, November 8, a Friday. That was the day my parents had left Seattle to go home. Ted had called me late that night. I had tried to reach him earlier but there was no answer. I had fallen asleep on the couch and when he called, I had a hard time waking up. He had gotten impatient with me and almost hung up. I kept saying, "Wait a minute, wait a minute," and then when he waited, I had nothing to say. He said to call him in the morning. It was about 11:00 P.M. here, so it would have been midnight in Utah. That was almost proof that he hadn't been out abducting women that night, wasn't it?

My bishop called me at work the next morning. He had told Hergesheimer how upset I was by what I read in the Salt Lake papers and suggested that authorities in Utah be contacted. Hergesheimer agreed to call Utah and let me know. Time dragged on. My bishop called a second time and there was still no word. At last I called Hergesheimer myself. He told me that people in King County had been so busy killing each other off that he hadn't had time to call Salt Lake City.

Christmas was coming and I was going home to Utah as usual. I could no longer get a whole night's sleep. I would wake up about two or three in the morning and toss and turn until the sun came up. I sometimes wondered if I was possessed. As the sleepless nights stacked up, my mental state got worse. I was afraid I would be murdered in Utah. I could visualize Ted finding out that I knew the truth. *He will murder me*, I thought, *but first he will murder Molly in front of me, and then my mother and father.*

During one awful night, I decided that I would call my dad. He had friends on various police forces; maybe he could help me. I waited until it was 6:00 A.M. in Utah. Maybe he would be up by then. His groggy voice told me he'd been asleep.

"Hello, Dad. This is Liz. . . . I need help. I'm scared that maybe Ted's involved in those murders in Utah. I wondered if maybe you could discreetly contact someone on the police force and they could check him out . . . ?"

There was total silence on the other end of the line. I thought maybe he'd gone back to sleep. But then, sounding absolutely appalled, he asked me why I would think such a thing. I fumbled to explain. He listened, and when I was through there was another long silence.

"You have to be absolutely certain before you contact the police," he said. "You would ruin his career if you were mistaken. Are you that sure?"

When I said no, he declined to get involved and we hung up. I got out of bed and plugged in the Christmas tree lights. I wrapped myself up in the afghan my mom had made for me. I sat in the rocking chair that had been my grandma's and stared at the lights on the tree.

As our plane circled over Salt Lake City, I was numb from lack of sleep. Ted was going to meet us and drive us to Ogden, but when we walked into the terminal he wasn't in sight. *Late as usual*, I told myself. Then suddenly he was there. He threw his arms around me and we rocked back and forth. I had forgotten how good it felt when he hugged me. Then a hug for Molly and then another hug for me. Then Molly and I hugged each other just to round things out.

We walked arm-in-arm down the concourse. "It looks like you brought some extra bags," he said, indicating the dark circles under my eyes.

Liz, Ted, and Molly on vacation to visit family. Ogden, Utah, 1970

Molly "learning to ride" Ted's bike. Green Lake, Seattle, 1970

Molly and Ted. Green Lake, Seattle, July 1970

Ted and Molly. Green Lake, Seattle, July 1970

Molly and Ted watching the "veg-o-matic man" at the Washington State Fair.
Puyallup, Washington, 1970

Molly and Ted baking cookies. Green Lake, Seattle, 1970

Waiting to go waterskiing. Flaming Gorge, Utah, 1970

Ted swinging Molly in the water. Flaming Gorge, Utah, 1970

Molly and Ted fishing for rainbow trout. Flaming Gorge, Utah, 1970

Visiting family. Ogden, Utah, 1970

Ted delighting Molly by jumping onto the already moving carousel.
Seattle Center, 1970

Molly and Liz at the Pacific Science Center. Seattle, 1970

Molly and Ted, celebrating Christmas. Green Lake, Seattle, 1970

Ted turns Molly's world upside down for Christmas. Green Lake, Seattle, 1970

Ted during our first camping trip. Pacific Northwest, 1970

An unhappy Ted who just woke up from a nap. Green Lake, Seattle, 1971

Ted in Wyoming on the way to Flaming Gorge, Utah. 1971

Molly's fifth birthday. Ted made the banner. Look past the '70s floral slipcover and note kitty Loretta wearing Molly's tinfoil birthday crown as a necklace. Green Lake, Seattle, 1971

Ted making rain for Molly and friends. University District, Seattle, 1972

Molly and Ted driving the boat. Flaming Gorge, Utah, 1971

Ted and Liz. Hood Canal, Washington, 1973

Ted and Liz get warm after a day at Snowbird. No skiing, as the lines were too long.
Ogden, Utah, December 1974

Christmas. Ogden, Utah, 1974

Ted and Molly at Grandad and Granny's house for Christmas.
Not sure how to handle the uncomfortable touching. Ogden, Utah, 1974

Ted tickling Molly. Liz hoping her secret call to the police is never revealed.
Ogden, Utah, December 1974

Molly and Ted at Christmastime. Hardware Ranch, Utah, 1974

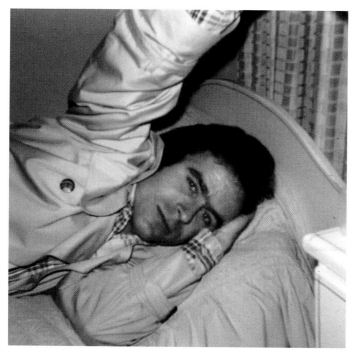

Ted taking a nap on Liz's childhood bed at Christmastime. Ogden, Utah, 1974

Molly putting barrettes in Ted's hair during his Seattle visit, just months before his initial arrest. University District, Seattle, June 1975

Ted and Molly wearing their hippie clothes. University District, Seattle, 1975

No longer worried after two police jurisdictions have checked
Ted out—one of them twice. Flaming Gorge, Utah, July 1975

Ted at Hood Canal, Washington. 1973

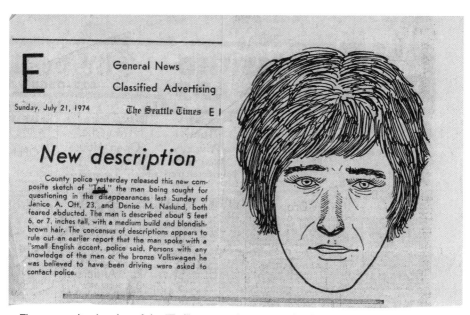

General News

Classified Advertising

Sunday, July 21, 1974   The Seattle Times E I

New description

County police yesterday released this new composite sketch of "Ted," the man being sought for questioning in the disappearances last Sunday of Janice A. Ott, 23, and Denise M. Naslund, both feared abducted. The man is described about 5 feet 6, or 7, inches tall, with a medium build and blondish-brown hair. The concensus of descriptions appears to rule out an earlier report that the man spoke with a "small English accent, police said. Persons with any knowledge of the man or the bronze Volkswagen he was believed to have been driving were asked to contact police.

The composite drawing of the "Ted" suspect that a coworker handed Liz. Seattle, July 1974

"How unkind of you to notice," I said. We both laughed. We collected my real bags, skis, poles, and boots, and we were off.

Before we drove to Ogden, Ted wanted to show me his apartment and the law school and the places he hung out. I couldn't have been more relieved sitting next to him in the car, laughing, talking, enjoying his company. I could understand why my dad was so stunned by my early morning phone call. As we walked into Ted's apartment, the phone rang. It was my dad.

"Are you all right?"

"Oh yes," I answered, "everything is just fine."

The holidays were wonderful. We spent the days going to Ted's favorite places in Salt Lake City. We visited friends and relatives. Once again, I realized what a gift Ted had for being at ease in social situations. I still watched his every move, but what I saw was Ted playing games with Molly, carrying my niece on his shoulders, helping my mom in the kitchen. Hardly the actions of a madman. The shadows were lifting, and I thanked God for the peace of mind I was beginning to feel again.

But there were bad times, like the day we went skiing. It started off on a Laurel and Hardy note. We loaded our skis on the back of Ted's VW while it was still in my parent's garage, and when we backed out, the tips of the skis caught on the top of the garage door and pulled the whole ski rack off the car. We looked at each other and laughed—the sophisticated skiers off on a jaunt!

We drove to Snowbird, a first-class resort east of Salt Lake City. Unfortunately, it looked as if half of California had come to Snowbird for Christmas break.

"They'd have to pay me to stand in those lines," Ted said. We decided to have lunch in the lodge and skip the skiing. We had to park in an outer lot, but that was okay because the resort sent big, open trucks around to pick people up and take them to the lodge. As we sat down in the truck on a bale of hay, a young, attractive woman started a conversation with Ted. He was so charming; she was soon telling him that she was from California and that she had come to Utah alone to do some skiing. I found myself thinking how easy it would be to trust this man, to go with him and die.

I didn't have much to say over lunch: I was fighting those feelings again. Ted was watching a bunch of teenagers horsing around. He dubbed the boy the girls were paying the most attention to "the James Dean of Midvale." Midvale was where Melissa Smith had disappeared. Would a time ever come when everything didn't remind me of murder?

We drove back to Ted's apartment. I had the urge to rip open his drawers and turn them upside down and pull everything out of the closet so I would know there was nothing there to worry about.

Ted had a little blue bottle of liqueur he said a woman who lived downstairs had made. "Here, have a taste," he said, holding the bottle out to me.

"No thanks," I said. I knew it was a knockout potion.

"You'll like it—just have a sample." He walked toward me holding the bottle in front of him. My mind was racing.

"No, I don't want any. I don't trust homemade stuff."

"It's okay. She makes it all the time. Here, just smell it." He thrust the bottle under my nose.

"I don't want to just smell it," I said and moved away from him, ready to flee.

"Suit yourself," he said, and took a big swig. The problem—as usual—was me.

I flew back to Seattle feeling better. My obsession with murder was gone, leaving as mysteriously as it had arrived. Ted would be flying to Seattle in two weeks at his semester break. I was genuinely looking forward to having him with me.

The first Sunday after I got back, I went in to tell my bishop the good news: My prayers had been answered. He was clearly happy for me, but he still thought I should check with the King County Police to make sure they had notified Salt Lake City. What for? I was irritated. Isn't an answer to a prayer an answer to a prayer? My bishop thought I should stamp out all doubt; otherwise it might linger in a corner of my mind and fester and then . . . well, it might start all over again. He was probably right. But I knew for sure that I wasn't going to call Hergesheimer again. This time, I was going to call Salt Lake City.

I put it off as long as I could. I was feeling so much better, why stir the pot again? Ted would be here in a couple of days, though, so I'd better get it over with. I slipped away to the same phone booth I'd been using to call Hergesheimer and called Information in Utah for the number of the Salt Lake Homicide Division. I was shaking as much as I had been the first day I called the police. A woman answered.

"I'd . . . like to speak . . . to someone who . . . knows about the woman who . . . escaped from a Volkswagen, you know, by a shopping center . . ."

"Just a moment please." She put me on hold. *Figure out what you're going to say, for Godsakes,* I told myself. Instead, I stared blankly at the dialing instructions on the phone.

She came back on the line. "May I ask who is calling?"

"Oh . . . I . . . I don't feel that I can say. But it's real important." My voice was cracking, and I could feel the tears backing up. "I'm calling from Seattle and I just really need to talk to someone there."

She put me on hold again. I rummaged in my purse for a Kleenex. Not only was I crying, but now my nose was running.

Great, just great. I would sound like a sniveling idiot.

"Captain Hayward here."

I jumped. Then I started one of my long, rambling sentences about my friend and his Volkswagen and where he lived and where he moved to.

Hayward cut me off. "I think we've already investigated him. What is his name?" When I told him, he said, "We looked at him a few months ago when your police up there contacted us. He looked okay. Weren't you just here for a vacation?"

How did he know that?

Hayward asked me what happened. What happened when? I was confused.

"Well, we had a nice vacation," I said. "Nothing seemed wrong."

"Then why are you calling today? What has happened?"

"Well . . ." I was asking myself the same thing. "I was just worried," I said.

"Well don't worry. We checked him out. There is nothing there to lead us to believe he is anything more than just a law student."

I finally gave Hayward my name, which of course he must have known, and then I hung up, feeling like a fool. I stared at the phone. It had to be the dirtiest I had ever seen. I hoped I didn't get a disease from it. Then I remembered that I had called Salt Lake City because Hergesheimer had let me believe that he hadn't. What a creep!

As soon as his finals were over, Ted was to catch an evening flight to Seattle. But I got a phone call early that morning. Ted was crying and having a hard time talking. He wasn't happy with himself. I asked him if he had bombed out on his finals. "It's not that," he said. "I just can't seem to connect with people. Sure, I can hold doors open for women and smile and be charming, but when it comes to basic relationships I just don't have it. There's something wrong with me."

I wasn't sure what he was telling me. Two police departments had checked him out three times. I wasn't going to get into that again. On the surface it sounded very much as if he felt bad because he didn't have a girlfriend in Salt Lake City and wanted to cry on my shoulder about that. I wanted him to come to Seattle. "Please come. We can talk and talk when you're here and we can hug and hold. You'll feel better, I guarantee it."

"No, I can't. I just don't think so."

"We can walk down the Ave and get a sandwich at Gilly's and maybe go see the Huskies play basketball."

"I don't know. I'll call you back," he told me. And he did call back—twice. Once to tell me he was coming; the second time to tell me he wasn't. After we talked a bit, he changed his mind again and said he would come.

When I picked him up at the airport that night, he was happy and confident. It was hard to believe he had been in the throes of indecision all day. He was carrying a brochure from a ski resort in Aspen. A man sitting next to him on the plane, a salesman for dental equipment, had been on a ski trip to Colorado and had given Ted the brochure. Ted was also carrying late Christmas presents for Molly and me.

It was a marvelous visit. I no longer watched his every move, but just enjoyed the things about him that made me love him. At moments I would get cold sweats thinking about what I had done to him by calling the police; but then, how would he ever find out?

In March 1975, the remains of Lynda Healy, Susan Rancourt, Roberta Parks, and Brenda Ball were found, all less than twelve miles from where Jan Ott and Denise Naslund had been found.

In April, the unthinkable happened—I turned thirty. I had made such a big deal of the onset of old age that I received five bouquets of flowers on that day. My house looked like a florist's shop. My parents,

Ted, my coworkers, the guys who lived upstairs, and a skiing buddy had all tried to ease the transition with flowers. Angie was back from a long trip to Europe and was staying with me temporarily. As she put it, I was another year closer to menopause. What a bummer! I had thought by the time I was thirty I would be happily married and have lots of kids. I had no one to blame but myself, so I had better get on with my life.

One day in early June, I straggled into the house after work and found Molly there, all sly grins. She was home by herself for two hours each day after school now, and I was pleased with how responsible she was. This day there seemed to be something going on.

"Come into my room for a minute," she said. I didn't know what to expect. I couldn't see anything special in her room.

Suddenly, two arms slipped around me from behind. For a split second I froze in terror. It was Ted. My knees buckled and he had to hold me up. "I had no idea you were coming," was all I could say.

He and Molly were pleased with themselves and their surprise. "I'm too old for this," I told them. "Please, no more surprises."

Ted stayed for almost a week. He had brought his raft and we went rafting on Green Lake a couple of times. It bothered me that his front license plate was propped up inside the car. But I refused to worry. When Ted said it had fallen off, that was enough for me.

Near the end of the visit, Ted called a friend who was going to be driving to Utah in August. He arranged for the friend to bring Ted's little brother to Salt Lake City. When I found out the friend was a woman who had a son about his brother's age, I thought that was so cozy it stank, and I told him so.

"Look," he said, "I didn't drive all the way up here to see her. I came to see you. I love you. You have friends that are men. Can't I have friends who are women?"

It was logical and reasonable, but I was still jealous. When Ted would get mad at me, he would tell me that I was insatiable, that no amount of his time or his love would ever be enough for me. I knew he was right, and I spent a lot of time going over and over my life trying to figure out when the plug had been pulled that had left me a hollow shell. Maybe it was in the college years or maybe it was in my marriage. I prayed to God that I would someday be a whole person, and I still thought the way to do this was to marry Ted.

I went back to Utah in late July. I knew that this was the turning point, that Ted and I were going to get married or break up. The first night I was there, Ted and I sat up late at my parents' kitchen table, talking and drinking. I asked him if he was still stealing things. When he waffled with a nonanswer, I exploded.

"You have a great future ahead of you and you jeopardize it with your stupid actions! Maybe you can't control it. Maybe you're a kleptomaniac." He looked stunned.

"The last thing I need is more problems," I went on. "If you got caught stealing, I wouldn't stand by you for a second."

"I get so tired of having nothing. You don't understand," he said, "because you've never had to go without."

"I've never had to go without because I work hard." I was angry. "I don't go without, but you don't see me furnishing my house with the best of everything." On and on I went, my motor mouth completely out of control. "If you're going to continue to steal, I don't want anything to do with you." The next morning, I woke with a hangover, going over the things I'd said. His stealing really did bother me, and I really did mean the things I'd said. I just wished I hadn't been drunk when I said them.

Later that day, we drove to Flaming Gorge National Recreation Area in Wyoming to meet the rest of the family, who had driven over earlier. I was trying to be cheerful. Ted said, "You know, I don't understand you. One day you act like I make you sick, and the next day you act like everything is fine."

I tried to apologize without backing down. "I want the best for you—for us," I said. "It scares me that you would gamble it all for a few material things." I thought of the gamble I had taken by going to the police. If Ted ever found out, that would be the end of us for sure.

At Flaming Gorge, we put our problems aside and enjoyed the sun and scenery. The fishing was terrible. We had been out in the boat for hours and hadn't caught a thing when my mother suddenly shouted, "I've got one! I've got one! Get the net!" Her pole was jerking and bending like there was a twenty-pounder on it, when Ted bobbed to the surface. He had slipped out of one side of the boat unnoticed, swum under it, and grabbed Mom's line. We all laughed about the "one that got away."

Ted and I had to leave the park early so he could get to work. On the way back we were talking about how our dads would never stop at scenic viewpoints or points of interest when we were kids, so when we saw a lovely river out in a cow pasture, we stopped the car and hiked over to it. Walking into the trees behind Ted, I was suddenly very scared and had an ominous feeling. The mosquitoes were huge and thick by the water.

"Let's go back," I said, swishing the bugs away.

"No, come with me." His voice sounded flat and hollow.

"Maybe our dads knew something we don't," I said and turned and hurried back to the car. Would I ever be normal again?

The day I was to fly back to Seattle, Ted and I sat on my parents' back lawn and talked about "us." I told him that I didn't want to continue this long-distance relationship, that I wanted to get married soon. To my surprise, Ted said, "Let's do it at Christmastime, then."

We got all excited talking about it and rushed in to tell my parents who were in the kitchen. Our great announcement was met with silence.

Ted was devastated. We went for a walk in the foothills. "I thought your parents liked me. I thought they would be happy we were finally going to do it."

I was confused. My dad and I had talked once, briefly, about my early morning phone call to him. I had told him that both the King County and Salt Lake City police had checked Ted out and found nothing. Had Dad told Mom about that call? Was he still worried about Ted? I was so sure the problem was in my head, and now I had planted seeds of doubt in my father's head too.

I flew back to Seattle and the next day I gave notice at work that I would be quitting at Christmas. My boss—a man not given to offering unsolicited advice—told me he thought I was making a mistake by marrying Ted. He thought Ted was a nice guy, but too much of a "climber" to pay attention to my needs. I was annoyed.

I called Angie and told her about my plans. "I sure hope you know what you're doing," she said. Now I was irritated that nobody seemed to be happy for me.

On August 16, I drove down to the Bundys' cabin on the lake to meet Ted's aunt who was visiting from back East. During the course of a conversation, Ted's mother mentioned that Ted had given his little brother a bicycle the week before when he was visiting Ted in Salt Lake City. She talked about how hard it was to get it home on the plane. I only heard half of what she said. I had given Ted a choice between me and stealing. That bicycle had to be stolen.

I left early and called Ted the minute I got home. No answer. I called all evening without getting him. The fact that he wasn't home at one in the morning made me madder. I called him early the next morning and there was still no answer. I didn't get hold of him until the next night. By this time, I was furious. I waded into him about the bicycle. "I won't marry you unless you straighten yourself out," I told him.

I expected him to defend himself, to try to make things right again, but he seemed confused about why I was so mad. He had been sleeping when I called, and he seemed disoriented. As we talked, I became aware that he sounded relieved that I was mad enough to call off the wedding. Just before he hung up, he said, "I want you to know that I'll always love you."

I lay down on the couch. I was so mad I was shaking, but at the same time I felt freer than I had in years. "You can just go to hell, Ted Bundy!"

CHAPTER ELEVEN

Ted phoned me more than usual after our big breakup, but our conversations had a dreamlike quality about them. We both said that we loved each other and always would. We both acknowledged that we had had an important effect on each other's lives, but we knew now that we would never get married and that our lives would grow in separate directions.

The thought of never making love to him again, of never window-shopping with him on the Ave, of never having family tickle fights again left me undone. At the same time there was a certain deadness inside me that told me it really was the end, this time.

One day in September, I ran into Ted's former landlady, Freda, in a supermarket. She asked me if I'd heard from Ted lately, and I told her that we had broken up, but that he still called me.

"The funniest thing happened," she began in her German accent. "A woman detective was by the other day asking about Ted. *Ja*, they thought he might have something to do with those girls that were missing last year. Isn't that silly? I told the woman what a good boy he was. He always helped me so."

"Are you sure she really was a detective?" I said.

"Oh, *ja*, she showed me her identification before I invited her in."

"Was she from the King County Police?"

"*Ja, ja*," she said.

The next morning, while everyone else in the office was on a break, I called the King County Police Department and asked to speak to Hergesheimer. The man who answered told me that Hergesheimer no longer worked in that division. As briefly as possible, I explained what had happened last fall and about the woman detective who had been asking questions about Ted.

"Oh, we're just cleaning out our files and going over some old information before throwing it out," he told me. I knew he was lying.

"Could I talk to the woman detective for a minute?"

"I'll see." He sounded angry.

The detective came on the phone and told me her name, Kathy McChesney. Once again, I went over the story of my calls to the police and the results. She told me she'd been planning to call me. She asked if I had talked with Ted lately. When I told her I had, she asked if he had told me that he had been arrested after trying to evade a police officer.

"When?"

"August 16. He was arrested and charged with possession of burglary tools."

I looked down at my desk calendar. August 16 was the day I had gone to the Bundys' cabin. That was the night I had kept calling.

"Would you be willing to talk to me further?" McChesney asked. "We could arrange to meet after you get off work."

"I'd rather do it right now," I told her. I said I'd be at her office as soon as possible.

I told my boss that something had come up and asked if I could leave for the day. He took a look at me and said, "I don't think you should drive anywhere until you feel better. Is there somewhere I could drop you off?" I appreciated the offer, but I couldn't ask him to drop me off at the police station.

The office I was looking for had "Major Crime Unit" above the door. Inside was a narrow room with an appointment-desk-type window, not at all the way I expected a police station to look.

I told the receptionist I wanted to see Kathy McChesney, and after a few minutes a petite woman who was younger than I came through the door.

"Are you Liz? I'm Kathy. Come on in."

She led me through a large room with lots of empty desks into a private office. She carried a steno note pad. She started the interview by telling me about Ted's arrest. She said he was charged with possession of burglary tools, but that the things found in his car might better be used to bind or assault somebody. She asked me what had prompted me to call the police.

I went through the whole thing again. Every few sentences I would stop and say, "I know I'm wrong," or "I'm probably crazy." I was trying hard to lay out the things that bothered me in a straightforward way, but I was so twisted up with contradictory thoughts that I just couldn't. Kathy seemed to understand what I was going through. We talked about my relationship with Ted before I had begun to worry. She was surprised that Ted and I had been together since the fall of 1969 and that nothing had ever seemed wrong until July 1974, when the two women disappeared from Lake Sammamish. We talked about Ted's stealing things, and I told her we had called off our plans to get married because of it. She asked about our sex life. Even though she was a woman, I was no more comfortable talking about it with her than I had been with Hergesheimer.

I asked her about the things found in Ted's car when he was arrested. She pulled a photo out of her steno book and looked at it. She asked me if I had ever known Ted to wear a ski mask.

I hadn't, but I remembered the day I bought a ski mask. Kathy asked me if I still had it, and I didn't know. She asked me to describe it and I tried. As she asked questions about it, she looked down again and again at the photo she held. Then she covered up most of the photo with her fingers and asked me to look at the ski mask. This was awkward, and I couldn't get a good look at it.

Finally, she said, "Please don't tell anyone I showed you this," and she handed me the photo. Laid out on a flat surface were gloves, ropes, handcuffs, an icepick, Ted's old brown gym bag, a crowbar, the ski mask (which wasn't mine), and a pair of pantyhose with eye slits cut in them. How horrifying it would be to see a man coming at you with that pulled over his face! I kept saying "Oh, God," over and over, not knowing whether I was praying or swearing.

Kathy wrote down a list of dates and times of disappearances and asked me to go home and think about it. If I could place Ted anywhere at any of those times, I could rule him out as a suspect in that case.

Over the next few weeks I spent a lot of time at the King County Police Department. I told Kathy about going through my cancelled checks to figure out where we might have been on the dates she gave me, but without any luck. I told her about the day I went through his gas receipts and about stealing a package of his cancelled checks. She asked me to bring them in. She also asked me what credit cards Ted had and if he had ever used mine. When I told her he had, she asked me to write to the companies and ask them to release my receipts to the King County Police.

When I brought in the envelope with Ted's cancelled checks, Kathy and I went through them one by one. She pulled out the same two checks I had wondered about last summer, the ones from the rental place and the surplus store. She asked me what I thought they were for. My guess was handcuffs from the surplus store and crutches from the rental place. But I had bought Ted's yellow raft from the surplus store, and maybe he had bought something for the raft. I told her about calling the rental place to ask them about identifying the cancelled check, and she told me the police could find out what he had bought with it.

Kathy seemed amused that I had taken the checks. She told me she had been suspicious or jealous of men in her life but had never gone so far as to steal their cancelled checks. She obviously didn't realize how consumed by fear I had been. Not concerned, not suspicious, not jealous, but scared out of my mind.

We talked endlessly about Ted. She asked me about any other women in Ted's life and I told her what little I knew. Kathy wanted to know if Marcy, the woman he had worked with at Harborview, was a small woman with long blond hair. When I said yes, Kathy said, "I know her." They had been bridesmaids together a couple of years ago. Small world.

As soon as I learned that Ted had been arrested, I called my mom and dad. I hated telling them, but I wanted to make sure they didn't get further involved. They had been inviting Ted for dinner often and visiting him in Salt Lake City. Mom was the one who remembered that they had been in Seattle at the time one of the young women had disappeared. Friday night, May 31, 1974, Ted had taken us all out for pizza, and when we got back to my house at 10:00 P.M., he was anxious to leave. He was supposed to meet us at my church the next day because Dad was baptizing Molly, but he didn't show up until the ceremony was over, about 3:00 P.M., two hours late. Kathy McChesney thought this was interesting, because Brenda Ball disappeared from the Flame Tavern in Seattle about 1:00 A.M. on June 1.

Ted continued to call me occasionally. Because things were so strained with us already, I didn't feel as if I had to act "normal." He asked me once if I could send him some money. I had loaned him money before, but I told him that I couldn't spare any now. He wanted to talk about us and how we could have avoided some of the mistakes we made. I didn't have much appetite for that kind of discussion, so he did most of the talking. Always after he called, I felt emotionally blitzed. This couldn't be the same man I was talking about with the police.

One day Kathy asked me again what I knew about Susan Phillips,

Ted's old girlfriend from San Francisco. When was the last time he had seen her? He had made a business trip to San Francisco in the summer of 1973 for the Republican State Committee. He had looked her up, but he told me it just proved that you can never go back. Kathy had a funny look on her face. "We've talked to Susan and to one of Susan's girlfriends. Ted and Susan were engaged around Christmas 1973." I didn't understand. "She spent Christmas here in 1973," Kathy said. "They were planning to get married. She also said that she visited Ted here for a while in the summer of 1973."

I was speechless. I was trying to remember Christmas 1973. That was the year I gave Ted a chess set and he gave me one, too. I had gone to Utah as usual. Ted told me he was going off skiing with some classmates. He had taken me to the airport, but he wasn't going to be back in time to pick me up. He had my car, so when I got back to Seattle, I was homebound until he got back.

I had been cleaning my oven New Year's night, when he appeared. He was so happy to see me and so full of loving words, that I teased him about having a guilty conscience. We went out to the Sandpiper, the tavern where we'd met, and necked in a back booth. That son-of-a-bitch!

Kathy told me that Susan had been in Seattle for a week in August that same year. I looked at the calendar on my checkbook: That was the week after Ted wrecked my car.

"Are you sure?" I asked Kathy.

"Susan sent me a picture that was taken by a friend. Do you want to see it?"

He had his arm around her. He looked very handsome. She was attractive, but not the gorgeous knockout I had imagined. I stared at the picture. They looked so happy. "Well," I said, "that proves he is a dishonest lover, but that still doesn't make him a murderer." I was both grateful and resentful that Kathy had showed me the picture, wishing I didn't know, but at the same time wanting every detail.

According to Kathy, Ted and Susan had a wonderful visit in the summer of 1973 and talked about marriage, but when Susan returned at Christmas, Ted was distracted to the point of being unpleasant. During a conversation about abortion, he had yelled at her and frightened her. When she returned to San Francisco, Ted didn't call or write. When she called him, he was cold. At last she told him to forget about getting married, and he said that was fine with him.

Kathy asked me if I knew why Ted would get so upset about abortion. For at least the tenth time since we had started, I extracted a promise from Kathy that the information I gave her would never go further than the file in her desk drawer. Then I tearfully told her about my abortion. Kathy looked as distressed as I felt. She was a professional, but she seemed to care about my misery. I asked her if I could have the picture of Ted and Susan together.

At first, she said no, but then she relented. "Now you have to promise that you'll never tell anyone." She made a copy, and I went home with a picture of that son-of-a-bitch and Susan in my purse.

CHAPTER TWELVE

I was missing a lot of work. My boss told me that he didn't know what was bothering me, but whatever it took to work it out was okay with him. One of the people at work pulled me aside and asked me if money would help with whatever was so heavy on my mind. He offered me a couple of hundred dollars, no strings attached. This kind of unconditional support meant a great deal to me. I was in constant touch with Angie and thanked God I had somebody to talk to. The police had questioned her a couple of times, but most of what she knew about Ted she got from me.

Several weeks after my first talk with Kathy McChesney, she told me that detectives were coming to Seattle from Salt Lake City and would like to talk to me. I was becoming more and more agitated as the police investigation heated up.

A few days later, her partner, Detective Bob Keppel, called me to tell me the men from Salt Lake City were here. I went downtown and was introduced to Ira Beal from the Bountiful Police Department and Jerry Thompson from the Salt Lake City Police. Beal went off with the King County detectives, and Thompson took me into a room with a polygraph in it. For a minute I thought they were going to ask me to take a lie detector test, but Thompson explained that this was the only room available.

"So how are ya today?" he asked me.

"Fine," I answered mechanically, then I changed my mind. "Well, really nervous, actually."

"How come?"

"I'm so scared by what's happening. Sometimes I think Ted is involved and then sometimes I just know I'm making a terrible mistake. I know that Ted's not capable of murder, but I get these awful feelings that it's true. . . ."

Thompson was looking at me as if he couldn't believe it. Hadn't anybody explained to him how unsure I was? He started to set up his tape recorder. "You don't mind if we record this, do ya?" Mind? Yes, I minded a whole bunch. He told me in an irritated way that to interview me without it made his job much more difficult. I didn't care; I refused to have what I said recorded.

He started the interview by telling me that Ted was a strong suspect in the November 8 attempted kidnapping of Carol DaRonch from a shopping mall in Murray, a suburb of Salt Lake City. This was the case I had read about in the papers so long ago, and Kathy and I had discussed it at great length. I told Thompson I was familiar with the case, but he continued to tick off the facts.

When he was finished, I told him that the DaRonch case had caused me to ask my bishop to call the police in Seattle and ask them to call the Salt Lake City Police.

We went over everything I had discussed with Kathy, from the length of my relationship with Ted to our sex life. It wasn't getting any easier to talk about. Thompson asked me about the clothes Ted wore—in particular, whether or not Ted often wore patent leather shoes. I thought that was funny, picturing Ted in black patent leathers with taps on the bottom and told him no. A couple of times during the interview, Thompson came back to the shoes. "He was pretty big on patent leather shoes, eh?" he would say. I couldn't have been clearer. "No, not ever."

After we had talked for more than an hour, Thompson pulled out what looked like enlargements of driver's license photos. "Do you know who these women are?" he asked me. They were pictures of two young women, both of them blond, both of them attractive. He was holding the pictures at arm's length from me.

"No, who?" I said.

"Sorry, can't tell ya," he answered.

I wanted to know, but he wouldn't budge. Kathy had asked me if I knew who Becky was. I didn't have any idea. It turned out she was a girl who had lived close to Ted in the U District of Seattle. They had gone out a couple of times and gone rafting once.

"You're kinda jealous, aren't ya?" Thompson said.

I couldn't argue with him.

The next day, Thompson and Beal came to see me. We sat in their car in the university parking garage and they asked me more questions. I had told Thompson that Ted had a fake mustache, that he had told me he wanted to see what he would look like with a mustache without going to the trouble of growing one. I described it as straight across and squared off at the ends. Thompson kept referring to it as "droopy." I described it again as squared off and Beal handed me a composite sketch drawn after Carol DaRonch's kidnapping. The man in the drawing had a droopy mustache. "No, it didn't look anything like this," I told them.

Thompson asked me if I had ever known Ted to have a metal rod or crowbar in his car, maybe with the handle taped. I was shocked. I did recall something I had not remembered in all my hours of questioning by Kathy McChesney. One night several years ago, Ted left my place to go home and study, but a little while later I heard someone coming up the front stairs quietly, as if trying not to be heard. I stepped out into the hallway and it was Ted. He had an odd look on his face, and he was retrieving a crowbar that had been under the radiator in the hall. The pockets of his coat were bulging, and on an impulse, I reached into a pocket to see what was in there. He backed away quickly, but I had pulled out a surgical glove. I couldn't remember now how he had explained it, but I remembered thinking how weird it was. I also told the detectives that Ted had taped the handle of my jack back in 1970, during the student riots. He told me to use it to protect myself if I needed it.

Even though it was a sunny September day, it was freezing in the parking garage. I was calmer that day, but I was still nervous and cold. Thompson and Beal sat in the front seat and I was alone in the back. At one point, Thompson turned to me and asked how I felt about Ted *now*.

Now? What had changed? I didn't know any more than I had before I talked with the detectives. I told him that I loved Ted very much and prayed and prayed that he wasn't involved in those murders, but that I just didn't know. That statement turned up later in several books and articles about Ted as proof that I was a real flake.

Thompson seemed exasperated with me. "I shouldn't do this," he said, "but because you've been so cooperative with me, I will let you in on something." He whipped out the picture that Kathy had already shown me of the things taken from Ted's car. I acted shocked.

"Now what do you think?" Thompson said.

"I just don't know," I told him. "But there is one thing I would like to know. Wasn't Carol DaRonch shown Ted's picture last year after she was kidnapped? In December after my bishop called? Or in January after I called?"

"You ask hard questions, don't ya?" Thompson answered. "I can't tell you that."

"You mean that now, after almost a year, you're going to ask her to identify Ted? I can't believe she didn't look at him months ago and say he wasn't the guy."

"There was a communication breakdown somewhere," Beal said softly.

Beal made some scrapings from the untaped end of my jack handle, telling me it could be old blood. They took the jack handle with them, gave me their phone numbers in Utah, and told me to call them collect if anything came up or if I had any questions.

That night when I got home from work, I found flowers from a florist. The card said, "I'll love you forever. Ted."

Ted was calling me more and more often. He had been baptized into the Mormon Church, he told me. I could interpret this, like most things that had happened lately, in two ways: If everything was normal, it would mean he had found a Mormon woman to convert for. But, if he was really involved in the crimes, it was the kind of thing a "trapped" man would do.

One Sunday in late September he called to tell me he was coming to Seattle. He said he was so broke that he was going to have to sell his Volkswagen, and he thought he could get much more for it in Seattle. When we had talked for about fifteen minutes, I told him I wasn't feeling good, that I would call him back in a little while.

I called King County Police and asked the operator to have Kathy call me. When the operator hesitated about calling Kathy at home, I told her it was an emergency.

Kathy told me that she couldn't advise me, but that if she were me, she would tell him not to come and that I knew he was being investigated.

I called Ted back and told him I knew he had been arrested.

"What? Just for speeding?" he told me, kind of laughing. "It was really nothing. I went through a stop sign and a highway patrolman picked me up."

"No, I know that you were charged with possession of burglary tools."

"They're harassing me. I was just out driving. When he stopped me, he went through my car. I just had a bunch of stuff that I'd collected. . . . He called it suspicious, and now they're out to get me."

"If it was just nothing, why did you run?"

"I didn't run anywhere." His voice was trembling. "The policeman got upset, that's all. I was just speeding, but he called it evading."

"Why did you have those things in the car?" I asked him.

"Really, Liz, it was just an accumulation of junk. I had the rope from the raft in that brown bag, you know. And a crowbar that is really handy for prying cars apart or like that. The search will never hold up in court. It was clearly illegal. Who told you about it, anyway?"

Ignoring his question, I asked him, "What about the pantyhose?"

"Oh that. I wear that under my ski mask when I'm shoveling snow. It's left over from last winter. I'm really going to get mad. Tomorrow, I'm going to talk with some people here and tell them to leave me and my friends alone. I'm really ticked off. Who told you?"

"I ran into Freda at the store and she told me a woman detective had contacted her, so I called the police."

"I'm calling Freda," he said and hung up.

A short time later he called me back. "What did the police tell you?" he demanded.

"Only that you'd been arrested and charged with possession of burglary tools."

"What did you tell them?" He was so agitated, I felt sorry for him.

"Only what I know. . . ."

I was glad he didn't press me. He said he was going to call Ann Rule, a middle-aged woman he had worked with at the Crisis Clinic. She was motherly and he had liked her very much. To meet her, you would think she was your average next-door neighbor, but she made her living writing stories for crime and true detective magazines. She was also close to the police, and Ted apparently thought she would be able to tell him how much they knew.

Again, he called me back, this time frantic. I wished for a moment that I could hold him in my arms and assure him that everything was going to be okay.

The days went by at incredible speed. Ted's arrest seemed inevitable. I called Thompson in Utah to see what was happening. He told me that he had taken Carol DaRonch to the law school to view Ted, but Ted hadn't shown up that day.

One Thursday Thompson called me at work at noon. "Are you ready?" he asked me. "Ted Bundy was arrested today, October 2, 1975, and charged with kidnapping and attempted homicide. "

I hung up and ran into the hallway. *Where am I going?* I asked myself. I went back into my office and closed the door. I called my dad's office in Ogden and got his answering service. I reached Mom at home and told her of Ted's arrest.

"I wish I was dead," I told her.

"Do you want us to fly up there?" she asked. "Do you want to come down here? Or send Molly here?"

I didn't know how I was going to get home from work that day, let alone what to do beyond that. I called Thompson back for more details. He told me that DaRonch had picked Ted out of a lineup, and his bail was set at a hundred thousand dollars. I asked him if he thought it would be in the Seattle newspapers.

"Not unless some eagle-eye reporter picks up on it," he said.

I called Angie at work, and she promised to meet me at my house. I told my boss about Ted's arrest, and he drove me home. I was shaking and crying so hard that he suggested we stop for a drink to calm my nerves. After two Scotches on the rocks, I did start to feel less scared.

The next few days passed in a blur. I told Molly that Ted had been arrested and was a suspect in the cases of the missing women. Even nine-year-old kids were very much aware of the disappearances. But even my responsibility for Molly couldn't keep me sober. I stayed at least mildly drunk throughout the day, and when the pain slipped through, I drank until I passed out. Angie was with me taking care of Molly. Molly's dad and his wife-to-be came up from Utah to help. I talked to Ted's mom often. She seemed to be taking it better than I was, but she hadn't betrayed him.

The headline in the Seattle *Post-Intelligencer* the morning after Ted's arrest was not quite what Thompson had prepared me for. *Ex-Evans Campaign Aide Held in Kidnap* was in huge type next to a picture of Ted. In smaller type was the line *Is Utah "Ted" the Seattle "Ted"?* There were six related articles, which I skimmed to see if they mentioned "tips from a girlfriend" or my name. They didn't.

One of Ted's friends had flown to Salt Lake City immediately after the arrest. When he returned, he brought me a letter from Ted. It said in part:

> *What can I say except that I love you. What can I do except want to touch you and hold you. What can I hope for except to hope that someday we can be together forever. . . . I can never hope to compensate for the sorrow and anguish I have caused you. This is what hurts me most. Be strong. . . . And as I am sure you have done, protect Molly from all this if it is not already too late. . . . I love you more and more. Forever and forever. This I know is true. God love you and be with you.*

I couldn't help wondering who was causing whom sorrow and anguish. If he only knew how untrue to him I'd been!

More letters followed.

If I regret anything in my life, then I regret not having shown you the deep love I have for you in a meaningful way to you. And should there be any desire that I want fulfilled it is a desire to prove to you beyond a doubt that my love for you is unshakeable and forever.

I didn't write to him. What could I say?

Dear Ted. Hope you're enjoying jail. I helped put you there. Love, Liz.

On October 23, I received from Ted what he called his "marathon letter"—it was about ten pages long. He told of adjusting to jail and preparing his defense, and he added words that tore my heart apart:

In this life we are fortunate to find one person to love and love completely. I am lucky because I love you in that way. Being in this jail has taught me this lesson. I think of no one else or miss no one else as I do you. . . . In this hour when my whole life is threatened, the only thing I regret losing is you and Molly. So I give you one more thing. It is the one part of me that cannot be taken away. I give you my love as deep and as powerful as any human being can have for another. I give it to you as the woman who has captured my very soul. Every last grain. There is no one to whom I could give my love for the rest of my life. My love for you is life itself. Without you there would be no life.

Ted.

He had added later:

I read over the last part of my letter to you. I want it to be clear. I write these words to you not because I want you to feel the same in return or feel obligated in some way. I just want you to know.

I was overcome with guilt. I had to tell Ted of my involvement with the police so he would quit sending me love letters and start hating me as I deserved. That night, after getting Molly to bed, I sat down to write him a letter.

The phone rang. It was Ted. "I was just writing you a letter," I told him.

"It's about time," he said. "I don't know how long they'll let me talk."

I interrupted him. "I have to tell you something important—something you're not going to want to hear."

I began shakily. "I've had some doubts . . . about you . . . for a long time. I got so worried that I went to the police myself a year ago." I paused to give him a chance to say something, but he was silent. "I knew you couldn't be involved, but there were all these things that bothered me, and I just couldn't stop thinking about it."

"Things like what?" he asked me. "What happened when you went to the police?"

I told him of my conversations with the King County and Salt Lake City police.

"It's okay," he told me. "You did what you had to do. If you told them the truth, then no harm has been done because the truth is good enough. The truth will prove me innocent."

— CHAPTER THIRTEEN —

Kathy McChesney called me at work and asked me to come down to the police station and pick up my jack handle and some other things of mine that she had. The scrapings from the jack handle had been tested in the lab and they were not blood. I had taken so much time off from work lately, I asked if she could bring them to me, but she was insistent that I come down to the police station. When I got there, she explained that her boss, Captain Mackie, had something he wanted to show me. We went into his office along with two other detectives. Mackie showed me what they had figured out from Ted's oil company credit card slips.

On a large pad of paper on an easel, Mackie had diagramed the locations from which young women had disappeared in Colorado. On the next sheet he had made a list of credit card slips from Colorado with Ted's signature. On a third sheet he had put the two together and showed that Ted had been in each location when the women had disappeared. I was stunned. Mackie told me that the license numbers on the slips varied. I remembered the visit Ted had made when the license plate of his VW was loosely propped up inside the car and told Mackie about it. Mackie told me all this was highly confidential information, and the only reason they were telling me was that they trusted me and wanted to impress on me the gravity of the investigation.

Next, they wanted to probe my sex life. I had discussed it with Hergesheimer, with Kathy, and with the two detectives from Utah, and now I was expected to go over it detail by detail again with these three men I hardly knew. My face was on fire. I stared at the floor, completely humiliated, as I answered their questions. How often? Where? When? What positions? Where are his hands? Where are your hands? Oral sex? Anal sex? Bondage? When it was time to go, I could barely move. I asked Kathy for my jack handle. "Sorry," she said, "we still need it."

That night Kathy called me at home to tell me that the Seattle *Times* was going to publish a story the next day regarding Ted's travels to Colorado and the murders there. She said a reporter had walked in right after I left and asked if his story was correct. What else could Mackie do but say yes? I found that hard to believe. I felt that I had been set up, and I was sick of being manipulated.

I was sick of thinking about anal rapes, strangulation with nylon stockings, beautiful healthy daughters torn away from their families. The world was a sick, sick place and I was profoundly sorry that I had brought my beautiful, innocent child into it.

When I looked in the mirror, I saw in my own reflection a similarity to the women who had died: the long brown hair, the pierced ears. Did they die because they looked like me?

Ted wrote to me:

> *My conscience is clear and my will to clear myself is strong. I cannot sense guilt which is not mine. . . . Liz, I know myself as no one else can, and I know I love people and life too much to destroy one living thing. This is the knowledge which gives me the strength to stand firm against all who challenge me. The world outside may have changed, but I have not.*

He seemed so together, and I felt so screwed up. He loved life but was locked away in prison. I hated life, yet I was free.

The newspapers were full of statements from Ted's friends,

111

outraged that this all-American boy was accused of these hideous crimes. I had double-crossed him and couldn't live with my conscience. I needed help. Two friends of friends had recommended the same psychiatrist, so I reluctantly made an appointment to see him. He asked me what I wanted from counseling. This threw me for a loop. There was nothing I could hope to gain from therapy; everything was cast in stone.

I dragged myself to the psychiatrist for several sessions because I didn't know what else to do. He suggested that I no longer have anything to do with either the police or Ted. He felt it would be impossible for me to have any peace of mind as long as I was being pulled in two directions. I told him I would have to think about it. That same day Kathy called and asked if I would come down to the police station and look at a shoe that had been left at the site where two young female hitchhikers had been found with their throats slit a year ago. I told her that my shrink had told me not to talk to the police or Ted anymore, and I didn't want her to call me again. She said she understood my need to protect myself, but she asked if they would be able to count on me later if they needed my help. I told her I didn't know.

On Thursday night, November 20, I got a phone call from Ted. "Hi! Guess where I am?" he said brightly. "I'm sitting in my attorney's office. When I walked over here it was starting to snow. It was so cold and fresh. I'm free!"

He'd been released on bond, but he didn't want to talk about the details. He told me he was going to have pizza and beer and more pizza and beer until he'd had his fill. Hearing the happiness in his voice made me happier than I had been for a long time.

Over the next few days, we talked and talked on the phone. My phone had developed an annoying click just about the time that Ted became a suspect. I wondered if it was tapped, but I told myself that I was being paranoid. Finally, it got so noticeable that I asked Kathy if the police had done anything to my phone.

"That would be illegal," she said. I knew that—but she hadn't answered my question.

In the back of my mind was the psychiatrist's advice to stop all contact with Ted, but Ted was so full of loving words. He told me that being in jail had taught him that the most important thing in his life was his love for me. I ate it up like a ham sandwich.

November 24 was Ted's birthday, and I called him at the house in Salt Lake City where he was staying with friends from the Mormon Church. Since he wasn't home, I left a message for him to call me, and when he didn't, jealousy took over again. He had mentioned a friend named Kim that his parents stayed with when they were in Salt Lake City. She had been a great support to him and had done errands for him while he was in jail. They had been "just friends" for about a year, he told me. As an afterthought, he told me that she was his lawyer's secretary. I tried to be mature when he talked about her. But when I couldn't reach him on his birthday, maturity went out the window. When he finally called, I was upset.

"For Godsakes, Liz, this is no time for jealousy," he said. "I need all the support I can get right now." He told me he had been invited to four different Thanksgiving dinners. I had sent Molly to Utah for ten days, and I was lonely. When he asked me what I would be doing at Thanksgiving, I tried to sound perky as I told him I was going out with friends, hoping to make him jealous.

On Thanksgiving Eve, I ran into Captain Mackie at the liquor store. I waved at him from across the room and left before he could ask me why I wouldn't cooperate with the police any more.

On Thanksgiving Day, my skiing buddy Len came to my place and we watched football and drank wine until it was time to meet

Angie and her friend at Horatio's, a restaurant on Seattle's Lake Union. I went into the bathroom to wash up, and when I came out Ted was standing in my kitchen. Len, who had let him in, was standing in the dining room, glaring. Ted looked pale and upset. I threw my arms around Ted. Gradually he relaxed and we rocked back and forth.

"Why didn't you tell me you were coming?"

"I was afraid you'd tell me not to," he said. He looked so vulnerable that I was sorry he was probably right. He told me that he had flown in late the night before and was staying with his friends Aaron and Debra in the Magnolia District. He asked me not to go to dinner at Horatio's but to stay with him. "It's important," he said. "I need to talk with you."

I didn't want to stay with him. I was a little bit scared. I told him to call me later.

"No, it's now or never." His voice was shaking. He walked towards the front door.

"Look, take the extra key to my car and go back to Aaron and Debra's. I'll call you when I get home." I didn't want him to go, but I didn't want him to stay. He told me he had his friend's car, but I insisted he take the keys to mine, to guarantee he'd be back.

At Horatio's, I drank most of my dinner and barely touched the food. Angie was the first to spot him—Ted pacing back and forth in the lobby, staring at us. I didn't know what to do. I went out and asked him to leave. Then I went into the ladies' room and from a pay phone, called my psychiatrist. He was away, and his answering service put me in touch with another doctor who advised me to call the police. But the last thing in the world I would do was call the police on Ted, *again*.

When I came out of the ladies' room he was gone. We finished dinner and Len took me home. He came in and checked the apartment to make sure Ted wasn't there. He offered to stay with me, but I sent him away.

Ted called from a phone booth and asked if he could come over. I suggested we meet somewhere for a drink. We agreed on Horatio's again. I called Angie and told her what I was doing. I was surprised at how strongly she objected. "I must see him one more time," I told her. I was lying, even to myself, to think this would be the last time. She made me promise to call her in a while.

As we were shown to a table in the bar, I glanced around to see if anyone was staring at us, but no one seemed to be. Ted's picture had been splashed across the front pages of the newspapers since his arrest, and I was afraid he would be recognized.

The conversation was strained at first. We stared at each other. He said that he had been afraid that he would never see me again. He asked if it would be okay if he held my hand.

We had always been so physical with each other, but now it was awkward. We tried to find things to talk about. Everything was different except for how much I cared about him. We sat sipping our drinks, when suddenly a man in a kilt appeared in the bar playing a bagpipe, music much too loud for the tiny room. He stopped right in front of our table and all eyes turned to him—and us. Ted and I looked at each other and began to laugh, our attempt to be inconspicuous blown to smithereens.

We decided to go on to the Edgewater Inn on the waterfront for another drink. As we walked out into the cool night air, Ted gathered me in his arms, and we kissed for a long, long time. He was a part of me and I was a part of him. Whatever was going to happen was going to happen to us together.

We drove in my car to the waterfront, and I remember parking the car, but the next thing I remember is sitting in the bar of the

Edgewater Inn, both of us crying. I knew I was drunk and apparently, we had been in the bar for over an hour, but I couldn't remember any of it. A year later, Ted wrote me about what we'd said that night.

He pleaded with me.

> *A million times I rehearsed this. . . . I pictured me on my knees begging forgiveness. I was going to tell you what a fool I was for my infidelities and I am. . . . For now, would it be wrong just to enjoy the love we have and forget everything else? Sounds like I'm asking you to play house, doesn't it? Maybe I am. I'm asking to pretend tomorrow doesn't exist. We'll sit here, drink our drinks, look out across the water, hold hands just like a pair of carefree lovers, just like we really were so long ago. It's just you and me. No courts, no detectives, no jail cells. . . .*

For just a moment I thought of all the people who would be disappointed in me, but I didn't care. "I love you, Ted Bundy," I said. "I want to be with you forever."

After we got back to my house, I called Angie and told her everything was "fine," that Ted was going to stay with me, and that I loved him with all my heart and soul.

"Have you lost your mind, Liz?" she asked me. "I don't believe this. That man may be a murderer—and you're going to let him stay there? Use your head."

"I have to do what I have to do," I said. I was offended that she couldn't understand what seemed crystal clear to me at that moment—that if there was the slightest chance that he was innocent, I couldn't and wouldn't let go. We made drunken love that night, and the next morning we stayed in bed till noon, making love, talking, laughing, reading aloud the letters he had written to me from jail.

We talked about getting married but discarded the idea. I was afraid that I was going to be subpoenaed to testify against him, and I was thinking that if I was his wife, they couldn't make me.

At last we rolled out of bed and began a round of doing our favorite things one more time. We strolled down the Ave, doing our version of the bump with our hips. Ted said he was going to call the news hotline at a local radio station and report that Ted Bundy was seen in the University District. Perhaps he would collect the prize for the best news tip of the week.

That night, as usual, I called Angie to talk. I was stunned when she told me that she was sorry, but as long as I was going to have anything to do with Ted, she didn't want to have anything to do with me. She said she could not support me while I made what she considered a very dangerous mistake.

"Well, fine," I said, trying to sound nonchalant, but feeling abandoned.

Saturday night we headed for the laundromat, and when we got there, Ted told me he was going to drop me off while he did some things.

"What things?"

"I think someone is following me. I want to make sure."

As I turned around to look, Ted barked, "Don't look, for Godsakes!"

I took the clothes out, and he took off up the street in my VW. No one took off after him. After a while he came back, still claiming that someone was following him but unable to prove it.

We went to the grocery store while the clothes washed.

"Damn it, there is somebody following us!" he said. "You shop. I'll be back." Again, he took off.

He was back a few minutes later, still with no proof. We loaded the groceries in the car and headed back to the laundromat. "Hang on," he suddenly said. We made a sharp right turn down a side street and then a sharp left. Then a sudden U-turn that took us back towards the first street we'd turned on. A black man in a black car, talking into a radio mike, came speeding by us. We fell in behind him, and he pulled into a Safeway parking lot. Ted pulled the car into the Burgermaster lot next door, jumped out, and approached the black man in the Safeway lot. I got out too, wondering what a bullet would feel like in my back. I half-expected to see Ted shot, then thought that if they shot Ted while I was watching, they would have to shoot me, too.

The man looked surprised. He was writing something on a clipboard. "Who are you? Why are you following me?" Ted demanded. The man didn't say anything. "Are you with the police? Or are you a private investigator?" Still the man said nothing, but he looked embarrassed. "Leave me alone," Ted said. "Just let me be." We went back to the VW and sat there until the man drove away.

"You should have stayed in the car," Ted told me. "This could be ugly. He could have been hired by the family of one of the murdered women. They want to see me dead. They may not wait for the courts." He said he had received obscene and vehement hate mail in jail.

When we got home, he pulled all the curtains, lit candles, and turned out the lights. He called his attorney and asked him to find out who was following us. Then we had a candlelight dinner. Later we played cards and drank wine by candlelight. Ted had never been a card player until he went to jail; now we spent hours playing the games he had learned there.

Ted's attorney learned that the police were, in fact, following us, and a semi apology was extended through the attorney. The policeman should have shown Ted his I.D. when we approached him. The game had rules.

Over the next few months, it developed into a war of nerves. The police staked out my house and followed us. They even brought in the police helicopter a few times. When Ted and I stepped out on the porch to go somewhere, so many unmarked police cars started up that it sounded like the beginning of the Indy 500. We would drive down the street singing "I love a parade" at the top of our voices as three or four cars followed along behind us. The only things lacking were crepe paper and a tuba.

Some days, when I was at work, Ted would go jogging in Discovery Park for the mere joy of watching the policemen pant along behind him. One day he came to my office, laughing heartily. Detectives Keppel and Dunn had been waiting for him when he left the house that morning. They had fallen in step with him and tried to talk with him, and when he wouldn't speak to them, they followed him down to my office. He had taken a detour into a building on campus that had a restroom with both a front and a back door. He said he hoped that Keppel and Dunn wouldn't wait more than an hour for him to come out.

Ted took me everywhere with him now, and that was what I had always wanted. I knew he needed me as a sort of cover, to counteract the image of "freak" he had been given by the press, but I was willing to play whatever game it was if I could stay by his side. He kept telling me how much he loved me and how important I was to him.

But nothing had really changed. One night we were at Aaron and Debra's, drinking beer and eating chicken enchiladas, when Ted got a long-distance call. I knew it was Kim Andrews, his Salt Lake City friend. He went into the bedroom to take the call, and I marched in right behind him. He paid no attention to me, so I went back into the living room and picked up the phone there. It was obvious from the conversation how deeply they cared for each other. "When are you coming back?" she wanted to know. "Soon," Ted answered.

I stormed out of the house and tried to unlock my car, but I couldn't get the key in the lock. Ted came out and asked me where I was going.

"Don't talk to me, you asshole!" I shouted. Ted looked around nervously to see if there were plainclothes police listening in.

"Come into the house," he said. "We'll talk."

He tried to take me back to the house, but I began hitting and pounding on him. I really wanted to break his goddamn jaw. "Leave me alone," I screamed. "I hate you." Finally, I got the door open, jumped into the car, pulled out, and left him standing in the dust. I thought he would probably follow me, and I wanted to get to my house and bolt the door before he got there.

To get from the Magnolia District to my house requires going through a tricky interchange of streets, and in my drunken state I took a wrong turn and found myself heading for downtown Seattle. I pulled over to figure out how I was going to go in the opposite direction and that's the last thing I remembered until I found myself in my garage.

I ran into the house. I could tell Ted had been there. I pushed the bolt in place so that he couldn't get back in, even though he had a key. I sat in the dining room with all the lights out. I knew he would be back, and I didn't know what I would do. Soon I heard his key in the lock. He called my name softly and jiggled the key furiously in the lock. I didn't answer and he kept it up. Finally, I said through the door, "Go away. Leave me alone. I don't want to see you anymore."

More loudly now, he started begging me to open the door, all the while jiggling the key. Then I heard the key break off in the lock, and at the same time, one of the guys who lived upstairs came to the head of the stairs.

"Leave her alone, man," he said.

"Fuck off," Ted told him.

"Hey, she told you to get out of here. If you don't, I'm calling the cops."

"Liz?" Ted called through the door. "If I call you from a phone booth, will you talk to me?"

I wanted him gone before there was more trouble, so I said yes. Five minutes later the phone rang. I let it ring for a long time. I almost had the strength to not answer it. Ted was crying. "The last thing in the whole world I want to do is hurt you," he was sobbing, "but over and over I wound you."

"Call me in the morning. I don't have anything to say to you now."

"Please, Liz. I'm sorry. Please forgive me. I love you so much." On and on he went. Eventually I decided that this man needed me so desperately that I told him to come back and I would let him in.

The next day, Ted sheepishly took the lock apart and removed the broken key. I kept it on my keyring for a long time as a reminder of what had happened that night.

It was Christmastime again and we led a parade of unmarked police cars to the Christmas tree lot. Sometimes the police were discreet, but sometimes they followed us so closely as to harass us. They pulled their cars in so close behind us at the lot I was tempted to ask them to help us tie the tree on the VW. Later we went shopping on the Ave and I bought Ted some corduroy slacks and a brown sweater as a combination birthday and Christmas present.

Ted had court dates in Salt Lake City, so he began a round of flying back and forth. For traveling, he assumed an alias, Christopher Robbins, from Molly's *Winnie the Pooh* books. He said that being Ted Bundy in public was just too hard. If he was relaxed and normal, people said he was putting up a good façade to hide his weirdness; if he got upset and irritated with the press or the police, people said he was evil; if he was jovial, people said he thought the idea of murder was funny.

I hated it when he was in Salt Lake City. Not only was Kim Andrews there, but I couldn't handle being alone very well. I had terrible dreams in vivid detail. Once I dreamed I found Molly battered and sexually mutilated. I held her on my lap and cried for help, but the police told me they were sorry: If I didn't help them, they couldn't help me. Another night, I dreamed that the killer was at my door, but when I looked out it was Kathy McChesney, so I opened the door. She began to strangle me, and in a flash, I realized that the killer had been a woman and that was why the dead women had trusted her. Then Ted jumped out of the closet where he had been hiding, saved me, and captured the real killer.

Ted called me often from Salt Lake. I found it easier to talk with him about certain things on the phone. Why had he gone to Colorado? How come he had never told me about going to Colorado? At first, he said he couldn't talk about it over the phone. I told him not to come back to Seattle unless he was willing to give me some answers. When he did return, he talked about Colorado with great reluctance. He told me that he wasn't doing well in school and that long drives gave him a chance to think about what was going wrong. He hadn't told me because he thought I would be angry that he was spending the time away from classes, and because it was costing him money, money that he sometimes borrowed from me.

On New Year's Eve, we were home before midnight. Ted was already asleep but I was still up when, shortly after midnight, there was a loud boom and the lights flickered and went out. The George Jackson Brigade, a radical group, had blown up a power substation near my house. The whole world had gone berserk.

When I was a little girl, I had been very upset to learn in Sunday School that someday Christ was going to come back to earth and it was going to be the end of the world. As I sat in my dark house those first few minutes of 1976, I figured now was as good a time as any.

Some of our worst chases with the police occurred when Ted was trying to leave town. He really disliked the idea of having his comings and goings monitored. He liked to take the 7:00 A.M. nonstop flight, so the night before he left, he would try to throw the cops off his trail. One night when we got caught up in a particularly desperate chase, Ted wanted me out of the car, so he screeched into my alley, pushed me out, and roared away. It was pitch black in the alley. The car that had been following us hadn't come into the alley, and I started to imagine that the men had left the car and were in the alley or in my garage watching me. As I crept up the side of the garage towards the house, my eyes straining to make out the shadows, I suddenly realized that the police would like to see me dead.

I could see the headlines:

Bundy Girlfriend Found Strangled
Bundy Charged with 1st Degree Murder

I started to run, feeling imaginary hands grabbing at my ankles and reaching for my neck. When I got into the house, unharmed, I knew it was only my mind tormenting me again, but still I couldn't stop shaking.

One night when Ted was in Salt Lake City, I got a phone call from a man who identified himself as a Seattle police officer. He told me he was calling because he was a Mormon. I checked him out in my church directory and called him back. He told me he hadn't been involved directly in the surveillance, but that he had heard it was getting pretty rough. He said there was a chance I might get hurt if I continued to be involved in the chases with Ted. He asked me to do what was right: to live by Church principles and be a good girl. The only thing I could say to him was that he didn't understand. After his phone call I felt tremendously guilty. Guilty of not living up to Church standards. Guilty of what I had done to Ted. Guilty of not being a good mother. Guilty of being alive.

As the trial approached, Ted spent more time in Salt Lake City. After having put him on a plane thinking that I wouldn't see him again until I flew there for the trial, I was surprised to get a call from him one Saturday morning saying he was in Seattle. He had been instructed by his attorney not to contact anyone, but he told me that his free life might be too short to skip the chance of being with me. I picked him up and we spent the rest of the day together. He told me that he had slipped into Seattle to take a lie-detector test that could be used in his defense. I thought that was wonderful. When he passed with flying colors, perhaps I would be able to let go of my doubts. When the results came back, they were inconclusive.

Monday, February 23, 1976, Ted's trial began in Salt Lake City. The charge of attempted murder had been dropped. He would be tried for attempted kidnapping. He had waived his right to a jury trial, believing that a judge, being more intelligent and better educated than a jury, would be better able to grasp what the hysteria in the press had done to Ted's chances for a fair trial.

I made arrangements for Molly to stay in Seattle with the family of one of her friends and arranged to take a week off from my job so I could go to Salt Lake City. At the last minute, Ted called and asked me not to come. My name had appeared on the list of possible prosecution witnesses when it was issued a month before the trial, but no one contacted me about testifying. According to Ted's attorney, the prosecutors called me "a real squirrel." His attorneys were afraid they might try to put me on the stand if they knew I was in Salt Lake City. I was skeptical. Salt Lake City was Kim Andrews territory, and I knew Ted would have a hard time balancing the two of us. She was to testify at the trial, and Ted had gone on and on about what a great friend she was to do this and what a sacrifice it was for her to be publicly identified with him. The day she testified, she was identified in the press as a "girlfriend" of Ted's. She testified that she had spent a great deal of time in Ted's apartment and that she had never seen a pair of patent leather shoes there, nor had she ever seen him wear patent leather shoes.

In early January, I had bought two cans of paint with the idea of painting my apartment on weekends. Six weeks later, I still hadn't finished, so I spent the week of Ted's trial painting. It was the kind of work suited to six-packs of beer and gave me the reason I needed to drink all day.

Ted's trial was big news. I kept the radio on all day, and Ted called me every night and gave me a play-by-play account. Carol DaRonch testified at length about the man she said had approached her at the shopping mall posing as a police officer. He told her someone had looted her car and asked her to go back with him to the car and check to see what was missing. After she found nothing gone, the "police officer" asked her to go with him to fill out a report. She had been suspicious of the man, but after he showed her a badge in his wallet, she got into his beige Volkswagen. Half a mile from the shopping center, he stopped the car and snapped handcuffs on one wrist. She resisted, and he was unable to cuff the other wrist. She said she tried to get out of the car.

"I was screaming, asking him what he was doing," she testified. "Then he pulled a gun, a small black one, and said he would blow my brains out. I got out the door and he slid across the seat after me. I was screaming as loud as I could and scratching him." Outside the car, she said, the man raised a pry bar in his right hand and tried to strike her, but she grabbed his arm. She managed to break free and ran out into the street, where she was picked up by a couple in a car. She testified that she was hysterical at the time.

When Ted's attorney, John O'Connell, cross-examined her, she admitted that she couldn't make a positive identification of Ted from the photos shown her by the police. She also gave testimony that conflicted with her earlier identification of Ted's car and admitted that she wasn't sure whether her assailant had a mustache. Ted told me that night that Carol DaRonch was indeed a very frightened young woman who had gone through a terrifying experience, but she was just plain wrong when she identified him as the man posing as a police officer.

Next, the older couple who had picked up DaRonch testified.

The woman said that when DaRonch appeared in their headlights with the handcuffs dangling from her wrist, she turned to lock her car door. That chilled me. It was like dreams I've had where I try to dial the police and the phone won't work, or I try to run away but the ground has turned into a treadmill. Fortunately, DaRonch had got the car door open before the woman was able to lock it.

On Thursday, Ted took the witness stand. He admitted that he had lied to the police and to his own attorney about what he had been doing the night he was arrested. He said that his "paranoia" about getting caught smoking marijuana had made him say that he had been at a nearby drive-in movie and had caused him to take off in his VW when the patrolman tried to stop him. He had driven for several blocks, throwing out a bag of pot and cigarette papers, and leaving the window open to air out the car. He was afraid that getting caught smoking pot would affect his law studies at the University of Utah. This was the first time I had heard this version. I wasn't anxious to analyze his story, but it didn't sound right to me. Of course, I also picked up on his statement that he had driven by a girlfriend's house earlier in the evening, but since the lights were out, he hadn't stopped.

Ted was the last witness. I flew to Salt Lake City that Thursday night.

Ted met me at the airport with his lawyer friend Aaron. His defense attorney, John O'Connell, had advised him not to go anywhere alone. Ted looked handsome and his spirits were high. He thought the case was going well, and he and Aaron discussed it endlessly over dinner in a Mexican restaurant. After dinner we went back to the airport to rent a car for me.

Ted and I drove to the university student housing where I was to stay with my former sister-in-law, Julie, and her husband and two kids. Molly and I had always stayed close to her dad's family. They were warm and happy people, and they meant a lot to me.

Ted went back to his place. We had agreed that I wouldn't go to court the next day. We were both worried that I would be identified, and I was afraid that my role in Ted's arrest would come out.

The next morning, he called before he left for court to tell me that he loved me. Julie and I sat around drinking coffee and making plans to go shopping. I had just stepped out of the shower when the phone rang. It was Aaron telling me that Ted wanted me in court right away.

"What's wrong?" I asked.

"I don't know. He just wants you there."

I threw on my wrinkled suit and with my long, wet hair dripping down my back, got a ride downtown with Julie's husband. Aaron met me in the hall, and we slipped into the courtroom and sat down with Mr. and Mrs. Bundy. The prosecutor, David Yocom, was delivering his closing argument. Ted turned around and gave me a half-smile. As Aaron had said, Ted just wanted me there.

I had felt as if all eyes were on me when I entered the courtroom, and it was a long time before I dared to look around. Judge Hanson was younger than I had expected.

Yocom was going through the evidence, saying it fit Ted Bundy to a T. He pulled out a chair and sat down on it, pretending to be Ted on the night of the attack, showing the judge how Ted had supposedly put the handcuffs on DaRonch.

Then it was O'Connell's turn. Sounding nervous, he told the packed courtroom that the evidence could fit a lot of people, not just Ted Bundy. The publicity surrounding Ted had created a monster, O'Connell said, a monster like things that go bump in the night or mutilate livestock. He hit hard at Carol DaRonch's suggestibility. She had picked Ted out of a lineup only because she had already been shown his picture several times. She identified Ted because she thought that was what the police wanted her to do.

When O'Connell was done, Judge Hanson read the instructions to the jury—even though there wasn't one—and recessed the court until his decision was made. As the courtroom was clearing, Ted leaned over to me and said, "That's Louis Smith." He said Melissa Smith's father came to court every day and stared at him. The guards frisked Smith every day, afraid that he would try to shoot the man he believed had killed his daughter. I looked at Smith and looked away, sensing the grief beneath his anger.

Ted and his attorneys left first; the press was waiting for them. I left with the Bundys by way of a back elevator, and we walked the short distance to O'Connell's office. There the Bundys were greeted warmly by Kim Andrews, a pretty blond about twenty-four. All I got from her was a piercing glare. When Ted arrived, he didn't introduce me to anyone, just let me sit by myself feeling left out and ugly in my wrinkled suit and uncurled hair.

We waited in the lawyer's office because it was thought that the judge might render a quick decision and Ted had to be available when he did. I spent a lot of time walking around the block or sitting outside on the steps of the building. Occasionally, when I would come back in, Ted would be sitting on the edge of Kim's desk and they would be laughing about something.

Finally, it was decided that there was no point in waiting around. Aaron left for the airport to fly back to Seattle and Ted and I dropped the Bundys off at the home of one of his church leaders where they were staying. Ted and I went over to the law school and ran into a couple of his friends. They discussed how the case was going. He didn't introduce me to them, either, and I wandered around the halls reading bulletin boards. When I came back, he told me we were going out to drink beer with his friends.

"Do I know you from somewhere?" I said. He told me he was

sorry he was so distracted and that he loved me and never wanted to be apart from me ever again. He kissed me and held me there in the law school hallway.

We went off to a tavern, and while Ted was playing pool, one of his fellow law school students asked me how long I'd known him. When I told her that we'd been going together since 1969, she said, "Now isn't it odd that he's never mentioned you?"

Later, alone with Ted in the car, I told him what she'd said and tried to make a joke of it. He grabbed my hand and said he was sorry, and that if he could only have another chance, he would shout his love for me from the rooftops. His voice was cracking.

"I love you," I said. "I'm sorry I brought it up. I know you love me." When we made our next stop at another friend's apartment, he introduced me as his fiancée.

His friend told me that he had been interviewed by the police. "They told me you talked to them, too," he said. "In fact, they told me some of the stuff you told them. Is it true?"

I didn't dare ask him what "stuff" he was talking about. Ted looked embarrassed. There were questions we didn't ask each other, by unspoken agreement. He didn't ask me why or what I told the police, and I didn't ask him about his connection to the crimes. After an awkward silence, Ted said he was sick of talking about police, witnesses, and trials. We left as soon as we could.

We went by Ted's place so that he could change clothes, then went back to Julie's. It was late and everybody else had gone to bed. Ted and I lay side by side in my bed and held each other.

There was no sexual energy in us. I fell into a deep but troubled sleep.

Early the next morning Ted nudged me awake. "Hold me, I'm scared. Hold me . . . please." His voice was urgent and childlike. I held his head against my chest and stroked his hair. I felt his tears on my body. I couldn't speak. I wanted to be strong and not cry, but the tears slid down my face. We held tight to each other and cried until Ted finally lifted his head and looked at me.

"Ugh! We need some Kleenex," he said. We were soggy messes with runny noses.

We got dressed and went for a walk. It was a cold, gray day. We held hands and walked along in silence; I couldn't catch my breath. We stopped and Ted ate breakfast at a place across from the campus. We would have spurts of conversation and abrupt silences.

Afterward, we walked back to student housing, then up towards the foothills. When we got to the zoo, Ted wanted to jump over the exit gate and go in, but I insisted on walking around to the entrance and paying the fee. It took one minute of watching the animals behind bars to freak Ted out. "What a stupid idea. . . . I should have known better," he said.

We wasted the day. At Ted's place there were telephone messages for him. He ripped them off the pad and took the phone in the other room to return the calls, leaving me out in the living room with one of his roommates. The guy was friendly and chatty, and I wished he'd shut up so I could tell if Ted was talking to Kim Andrews. Ted got done on the phone and decided to take a shower. The roommate went off to the store. I searched the pockets of Ted's pants, the garbage can, and the closet for the phone messages. I was afraid Ted would catch me, but I couldn't stand not knowing who he had called. I didn't find what I was looking for, but I didn't dare ask.

We went to a tavern where Ted ran into a couple of people he knew. Julie's husband was there and we talked for a long time. I called Julie and told her we'd bring home lots of beer and stuff to make tacos.

We parked in the grocery store lot, and as we walked towards the store, I could feel Ted's hand shaking in mine. As we pushed the cart around the store and debated what kind of beer we wanted—

he wanted his favorite, Mickey's, and I wanted Coors, which you couldn't get in Seattle at that time—I noticed beads of perspiration on his forehead.

"Oh, God," he said. "Every time I do something I wonder if it's the last time I'll ever do it. Like the shirts that we dropped off at the cleaners—what if I can't get them on Wednesday?" His voice was low and pleading. "I used to take everything for granted, but everything is so important. I love life. If I can't be free, I want to be dead."

I took his hand and led him out of the stuffy store into the cold air. We sat close together on a brick planter, not saying anything. I was thinking that maybe he should take the car and go to Mexico. Then I saw that that wouldn't help; life on the run isn't freedom, either.

"I want to get drunk," he finally said. "Absolutely roasted. Go finish the shopping. I'm staying out here." That sounded like the best idea I'd ever heard, so I threw in some extra beer and we stopped at the liquor store and got some wine, too.

Back at Julie's, we started drinking and cooking with a vengeance. I excused myself briefly—I had to get into my suitcase to find my Valium. Lately, I hadn't been able to "take the edge off" with just alcohol. I'd tried switching and combining wine, beer, Scotch, and bourbon, but nothing worked. A couple of Valiums helped immensely.

All of us pigged out on the tacos. After the kids were in bed, we smoked some dope. We watched Monty Python and I didn't understand most of it. I couldn't remember when I had taken the Valium, so I took a couple more. When the beer was gone, we started on the wine. By the time *Saturday Night Live* came on, I could hardly see. I lay across Ted's lap and he tickled my back for a long, long time.

Sunday morning, we got up very slowly. I drove up to my folks' house for midday dinner. Conversation was strained. My folks were horrified that I was still standing by Ted. I loved my parents very much that day for not trying to discuss it. I didn't stay long. I wanted to get back to Ted. I swung by his place and picked him up, and we went back to Julie's. There was nobody home. We lay down on the couch and kissed. Slowly we began making love, and for a few moments, the breathless excitement blocked everything else out and made things seem the way they used to be.

As Sunday wound down and Monday approached, the tension grew. We knew the verdict would probably come on Monday. We drank and watched TV and went to bed early. Monday morning, I popped out of a drug-induced steep to find Ted looking at me intently.

"I love you so much," he told me. I started to cry. I didn't want it to be Monday morning already. "Don't cry," he said. "Just know that I love you." He took me in his arms, and we tried to make love, knowing that it really was the last time, but it was pointless; neither of us could feel anything. It was like being paralyzed.

About nine o'clock, John O'Connell called and told Ted to get to his office immediately. A verdict had been reached. Panic-stricken, I threw on my clothes while Ted phoned his parents.

It was starting to snow, and the streets were slick. We stopped at Ted's place and he ran in to change his slacks. He came running out carrying his jacket, shirt, and tie. He changed in the car, throwing his yellow turtleneck sweater over the back seat. I dropped him off, found a parking place, and dashed up to the judge's chambers where Ted's parents were waiting. Judge Hanson was there, talking with Mrs. Bundy. I wondered how he must feel. Ted and his attorneys came in. He gave me a wink and a forced smile as he came through the door.

We went into the courtroom and took our seats. They must have turned off the heat in the old courthouse over the weekend, because the room was freezing. I recognized a man sitting behind the prosecutor as Police Captain Hayward, the man I had called from Seattle over a year ago; the man who told me not to worry; the man who had denied that he had ever talked with me. Jerry Thompson, the detective I didn't like, was sitting on the other side of the courtroom.

I stared at Ted's back for a long while. He was fiddling with his hair, one of his usual nervous habits. I liked the way his hands looked. Next to me, Mr. Bundy was holding Mrs. Bundy's hand.

We all stood up as Judge Hanson entered. After we were seated, the judge asked the defendant to please rise and step forward. I thought I might throw up. Ted and O'Connell stood before the judge. Hanson read the verdict fast: *guilty*. Mrs. Bundy let out a soft gasp and broke into tears. As if from outside myself, I saw that I was crying, too.

Detective Thompson had stationed himself at the entrance to the judge's chamber to take Ted away. There was another officer at the other side of the door. They were going to take him because of all the garbage I had told them. I had tried to tell them I was wrong, but they wouldn't listen. They were so desperate to solve their cases that they had taken a man who might be a thief and had made him into a mass murderer.

Ted asked if he could have a few minutes alone with his family. As he entered the judge's chamber the two detectives grabbed him roughly, pulled his arms behind his back, and snapped handcuffs on his wrists.

"You don't need those," Ted said through clenched teeth. "I'm not going anywhere."

As they frisked Ted, I leaned close to Thompson and said bitterly, "Revenge is sweet, isn't it, Jerry?" I wanted to spit in his face, claw his eyes out, hammer him. But I knew—everyone in the room knew—who was really to blame for this insane finale. I put my arms around Ted and my head on his chest. "I'm sorry, I'm sorry, I love you." He didn't respond. He was drenched with sweat. His spirit was gone. He was like a dead man standing up.

"Let's go! Let's go! Take him down the stairs!" the detectives were shouting. I couldn't look as they took him away.

CHAPTER FIFTEEN

After Ted was taken away, Mr. and Mrs. Bundy and I went directly to the airport. We had three hours to wait until the next flight to Seattle. I ended up in the airport bar where I drank and wrote Ted a tearful letter on the only paper I had, a savings passbook. The waitress asked me if I was okay. I didn't care what anybody thought. The people in the bar were talking about Ted's conviction. When the waitress came by again I told her she was wrong—Ted wasn't guilty—and she shouldn't blow off her mouth when she didn't know what she was talking about.

On the plane I kept drinking. Mrs. Bundy came and sat with me for a little while. She told me a little about the man who had fathered Ted but hadn't even stuck around until he was born. She told me about living in Philadelphia with her young child and the need to start a new life for herself and her son. She had moved to Tacoma and met Johnnie Bundy. They had had a small wedding. Ted was five years old, and he had stuck his hand in the wedding cake. "That's why I never discussed it with him," she said. "I thought he remembered."

A few days after I returned to Seattle, I got a phone call from Don Hull, the probation officer who was writing the presentence report on Ted. He wanted to know if I still thought Ted was guilty. Maybe it was just a matter of semantics, but I didn't think I had ever told anyone I thought Ted was guilty—not flatly. Hull read from Jerry Thompson's police report, that I had said that Ted frequently roamed around the neighborhood late at night and had a bad habit of jumping out of hiding places to scare me. I couldn't believe the distortion of what I had said. I had told Thompson that Ted had hidden and scared me a few times in all the years I had known him, but I had never said he made a habit of it. When I wouldn't confirm Thompson's report, Hull said he had heard I'd had a change of heart. It was a terrible phone call, and if I'd had enough energy, I would have been furious, but the conversation only left me more depressed.

When Ted called me a few days later, I told him about Hull's phone call, and he asked me to call Hull back and try to make sure he knew I didn't agree with Thompson's report. Ted said that his own talks with Hull had convinced him that there was no hope of a fair presentencing report.

I put off calling Don Hull back for a few days because I knew it would be bad, and it was. I dragged myself back to the same phone booth where many months ago I had called the police. As I sat there trying to figure out what I was going to say to Hull, I was overcome by anger. How many women died after I made those calls? If the police were so goddamn sure that Ted was guilty, shouldn't they be held accountable for the deaths that occurred after I called them in October 1974? Weren't they murderously irresponsible? I called Hull and told him I thought Thompson's report was slanted and full of inaccuracies. Hull dismissed this again, attributing it to my "change of heart," and I hung up. The inconsistencies in my thinking bothered me. *I am*, I thought, *capable of holding a hundred different points of view on any one idea at any one time. There is no real me.* That same day I had my first visit with a counselor.

That night I went home, got drunk, and wrote Hull a letter. Ted called just after I finished it. When I read it to him, he said it was impressive and persuasive. Among other things I wrote, *You call it a change of heart. I call it putting my head on straight.* Hull had been to see Ted a couple of times. He told Ted that he had spoken with Carol DaRonch and that she was ninety percent sure that Ted was the one. Ted was dumbfounded.

"A standard interpretation of 'beyond a reasonable doubt' given by a judge to a jury is 'if after a consideration of the evidence you are ninety-five percent sure that the defendant is guilty, you must acquit,'" he told me. "There is a 'reasonable doubt.' Not even Carol DaRonch could have found me guilty. I am not!"

Hull had asked Ted some questions about his "old girlfriend" Angie. Furious that she would portray herself as having an intimate relationship with Ted, I called Angie and gave her hell. She was horrified that she had been identified as an ex-girlfriend. She told me she had never talked with Hull, so I could only guess that the label had come from Thompson's report. Angie was so upset that she called me back the next morning and told me that if Hull did call her, she wouldn't speak to him. I sure missed Angie's friendship.

My life had changed so much that I couldn't believe it was still my life. I was spending most of my waking hours sifting through the past, reliving my mistakes. Sometimes I would bury my face in the yellow turtleneck sweater of Ted's that I had retrieved from the back of the rental car in Salt Lake City. It smelled like a mixture of Tide and Right Guard, a distinctly good and Ted-like smell. I missed him more than I thought possible.

The newspapers were full of stories about Patty Hearst. She and her SLA abductors had been captured in September 1975, and now in March 1976, she was on trial for helping the SLA rob a bank. There was much discussion in the press about whether or not she had been brainwashed. She had been kidnapped and physically, mentally, and sexually abused; but some people didn't understand why that would cause her to join with her kidnappers. I thought of writing her a letter, because I understood perfectly well what the power of fear could do to a person.

On March 22, Ted appeared before Judge Hanson to be sentenced, but the judge ordered him to the Utah State Prison for a ninety-day psychiatric evaluation. At first Ted thought there was hope. He knew he was a normal, healthy young man—not a murderer or a kidnapper—and he knew this would come through in any fair evaluation. The day he appeared in court I heard something on TV that made me fire off a furious letter to him:

> *They always make me grit my teeth, but this one got me on my glass jaw. They went on and on about the court proceedings and then said the judge had ordered that Mrs. Bundy and Bundy's girlfriend be allowed to visit with you in private. Since I'm up here and Judge Hanson was down there, I surmised there must be two girlfriends. Good old Kim. What would we do without her?*

This was the thousand-millionth time I had felt this way about Ted and another woman. Ted was Ted. He would never change. I don't know what I expected him to do about anything, especially now, but I unloaded on him anyway.

I discussed Ted and other women with my counselor at great length. "If it hurts," he asked me, "why do you put up with it?" The answers were the same as they had always been: Because I love him and because I'm stupid. I discussed the guilt I felt about calling the police in the first place, and the fears and doubts about Ted that had prompted the calls. I felt unfaithful to Ted discussing this with a stranger but saying my thoughts out loud to another person took some of the sting out of them.

I wrote Ted:

I am a mature (reasonably) person and can accept things as they are—if I only know how things honestly are. Of course, what I am talking about is your relationship with Kim Andrews. I don't like the way I throw up my defenses at the slightest possibility that someone is going to tell me something I thought I knew but didn't. It's like being emotionally shell-shocked. So, I have a deal to propose. Will you candidly tell me how it is? And whatever else there is to tell about things that might fall out of the sky to shock me. And for my part, I won't bring it up ever again.

His answer:

Kim Andrews . . . is a loyal and close friend. She has volunteered to do things for me which no one else down here has volunteered to do. . . . If she had replaced you, I would tell you. If I loved her and no longer loved you, I would tell you. But she hasn't and I don't.

I didn't feel a whole lot better.

My counselor was pushing me to open up in group therapy, and finally I took the plunge. I told the group I was dying of terminal loneliness, that my boyfriend who had been my whole life was in jail and now I had no one. We talked about the few steps I had taken to put my life back together. They asked about my daily routine. I told them that every day ended the same way: I drank, wrote letters to my boyfriend, and cried a lot.

One of the women, who was a recovering alcoholic, suggested that I probably wouldn't cry so much if I didn't drink so much. It had been her experience that she couldn't make any important changes in her life until she had cut out the alcohol, which she said distorted reality for her. I told her that that was exactly what I needed—a reality distorter. But I admitted that I couldn't seem to get drunk enough anymore, no matter how much I drank.

It was getting harder and harder to take the edge off. Sometimes I'd drink till I threw up and still wouldn't be drunk. At other times I would have one beer and it was as if I'd been hit between the eyes with a hammer. The hangovers were getting worse; usually it was the middle of the afternoon before I felt human. I told the counselor that I wasn't ready to quit, but that I would try to slow down. He told me that he didn't think any amount of counseling would help me if I didn't stop drinking. I thought he was overreacting. If I quit drinking that would just give me more hours to kill in the evening.

"You're a bright woman," he told me. "You're at a turning point. It's up to you to make the right decisions."

But I was worn out from making decisions. I wanted someone else to do it for me. When he suggested that I attend an alcohol recovery meeting, I was insulted. I took care of myself; I had a responsible job; I didn't leave my child at home while I ran around to taverns. I wasn't an alcoholic!

Without alcohol, my hands shook, my back ached, and my disposition was rotten. When the counselor told me that these were symptoms of alcohol withdrawal, I was shocked. I was totally unprepared for what life without alcohol would be like. I wrote Ted:

> I have quit drinking and I have discovered that by drinking I have only postponed all the hurt, agony and sorrow. I am feeling these emotions intensely now. It is so painful that the temptation to soften it all with a drink is very strong.

I was mad at the counselor for making me quit. I was mad at everyone. The counselor and the two recovering alcoholics in the therapy group were pushing recovery meetings at me. They said I'd find people there who were going through the same things I was. Fat chance. There was only one Ted Bundy and nobody else was dealing with what I was. Whenever I made arrangements to go to a meeting with one of the women, something always came up so that I had to cancel. But I wasn't drinking, and as much as I carried on about how miserable I was without booze, every day that went by without a drink was a triumph to me.

Eventually, the nagging I got from the group wore me down, and I made a contract with them to attend an alcohol recovery group. It was in a rundown second-story hall in a slightly shabby neighborhood, and as I walked slowly up the stairs, I said to myself, "So this is it, the bottom of the barrel."

This particular meeting was for women only, and to my surprise they were all fairly intelligent, clean, happy women about my age. I listened to their stories about their lives when they were drinking as compared to their lives now that they were sober, and I could identify with the feelings of guilt and remorse and self-hatred that they talked about. They told me that if I didn't take the first drink, I wouldn't get drunk. I had never thought of it that way, and it seemed like the most profound thing I'd ever heard. They also told me they lived their lives and stayed sober one day at a time. I wondered if that would work for me; I was tired of reliving the past every day.

It embarrassed me to tell Ted about going to meetings to get sober, but I needed his praise and his opinions. He wrote:

> *You have every right to be proud of your success in stopping drinking. We both know how much alcohol was a part of our lives. . . . Your success is genuine.*

He cheered me on like a football coach and I loved him for it. And I tried to support him as well as I could. In our letters we fantasized about a new life for the three of us, a new life away from fear and worry, perhaps on a small farm or a cabin in the mountains.

His letters detailed the ninety-day evaluation.

> *Then there was the educational achievement tests. First there was spelling. "Spell cat," said our lemon faced school marm who didn't seem to think any of us could.*

In another letter:

> *I received a message today from the University Medical Center. It seems the EEG they did on me last week was inadequate because I was not relaxed. I can't imagine why I wasn't! After all, aren't handcuffs, chains and leg irons conducive to relaxation? I tried my best though. As I lay there in the dark, my eyes closed, I repeated over and over "I love her, I love her" with your picture in my mind. You are with me everywhere I go.*

It was in every letter.

> *The only reality I fight to preserve is you. You are my link to everything I hold dear. You keep alive emotions of caring and loving. I love you and Molly. . . . The psychologist gave me a test where pictures are shown, and a story was told by me about each picture. The last card was blank, and I was to imagine a picture. It was a picture of you in the kitchen and as I told it tears began flowing uncontrollably down my face. I miss everything about you.*

Then in May he wrote:

Not to my surprise, the combined results of all psycholog-
ical and medical tests show me to be completely normal,
a psychiatrist told me. He kept saying "Very interesting."
He also said that he believes me when I say I didn't do
it, but being a loyal employee of the state, he asked me if
it was possible I had forgotten it all. They never give up.

And in another letter:

They have reached the end of their proverbial rope and
are now insinuating that I am very complex and hard to
know which simply means that they have no basis to say
that x caused y kidnapping. The psychiatrist has been the
most honest with me. He has said on two occasions that he
can see nothing to suggest that I was in any way capable
of committing such a crime. . . . Both Don Morgan, my
probation officer, and Al Carlisle, psychologist, are anxious
to talk to you. I suggest you speak to them and be honest
with them but be careful. Morgan, for instance, made
reference to the "numerous contradictions in statements"
you made to the King County authorities (something
about composite picture similarities). I was not aware of
such statements and I really do not think they are in any
way relevant to the evaluation of me as a person. . . . I
should clarify something at this point. Nothing you have
said has hurt me. Your honest and forceful statement of
your opinions about me now, however, can be helpful. I
do have confidence in you.

Later in May:

This evaluation has reached the final impasse. Stalemate and I lose. He (the psychiatrist) is saying "I don't have enough information to predict your future behavior" which is bullshit. (Or "please confess, it would make everything so simple.") What he is saying is that he cannot predict violence, my tests are too good, but he is too much of a coward to forecast peaceful behavior. I think I can pry him off his rock, though.

On June 14 he wrote:

The tension builds each day as sentencing approaches. . . . I am in no way mentally prepared to accept anything the judge imposes, least of all commitment. . . . I am really not as brave as I would like to make myself believe. . . . When I think of years without you I see an eternity in hell. I need you and my freedom too dearly to accept commitment to prison with no more emotional response than I would have to spoiled milk. There is no denying the life and death significance of next Tuesday.

The last letter he wrote me before he was to be sentenced was the worst.

Time and circumstances have converged; all our lives have been focused on one day. For you and I, it has all come down to this final letter, the last letter you will receive before I am sentenced next Wednesday. At such a time, I am unable to choke back the urge to cry or hold back the tears. It is not that what I have to say is so sad; rather it is the realization that I may not be saying it again which makes me emotional. I would like this to be my finest, softest love letter. I wish each word could kiss you.

He went on to tell me that I was the woman he loved and had "loved exclusively for years," that I had given his life "the meaning which gives living beauty and dimension," that I was the woman who made him know "what it is to be a man," the lover who had taught him "the secret thrills of my sexuality," a mother who showed him "the joy and fulfillment of raising a child."

I would not change places with any other man in the world. I consider you a miracle in my life and in spite of the disaster we have suffered, I would not for a moment ever wish for another woman. You are the most loving and lovely woman I have ever known. You are in my mind constantly. No words can express adequately the dimensions of my feelings. I shall love you forever and forever in my dreams. I shall love you with every long-haired beauty I see. I shall love you with every clear blue sky. I will love you til my last breath. There can never be any goodbyes for you and I. No parting because we are always with each other in spirit. No goodbyes, just I love you.

My reaction to this letter was so intense that I scared myself. This was the end that I had been trying to ignore for the last three months. I knew Ted would be sentenced to life in prison. What a cruel joke, "*life*" in prison. He would die in there, and I would be responsible for his death. God, how I regretted making those phone calls.

I had a list of phone numbers of people in recovery I could call if I was afraid of taking a drink. I had no desire to drink. I wanted to die, and I didn't know if it would be okay to call them under those circumstances. I didn't know how to ask for help. I pulled myself together enough to make arrangements for Molly to stay with friends, and when I was alone, I threw myself on the floor and against the walls, cursing myself for being alive. I was so hysterical when I picked up the phone and called one of the recovering alcoholic women I knew from group therapy that at first she couldn't understand me, but she listened and offered to come to my house.

I didn't want that, and I think I frightened her. She gave me the name of another, older woman and made me promise to call her. A part of me was sure that no one wanted to help me because I was loathsome. How could I call on a total stranger for help? I turned angrily to God. *Help me, help me, help me!* I demanded. The answer I got was to call the woman. Her name was Pat.

She was an oasis of serenity. She listened to me and talked to me about a loving God. She asked me how long I'd been sober, and when I told her it had been about seven weeks, she said that I couldn't possibly hope to feel together and sane all the time this soon. After years of anesthetizing our bodies and our brains, she said, we didn't have the ability to handle our emotions like normal people. I didn't want to tell her that I was still wrestling with whether or not I was an alcoholic.

We talked for a long while. She became my good friend in recovery, and I owe my life to her.

Bundy Gets 1 to 15 Years the headline read.

Convicted kidnapper Theodore R. Bundy of Tacoma was sentenced in Salt Lake City to one to 15 years in prison yesterday for the abduction of a young woman in a Murray, Utah, shopping mall in 1974.

District Court Judge Stewart M. Hanson Jr. passed sentence after Bundy, a former University of Utah and University of Puget Sound law student, made a tearful plea that his incarceration would serve no purpose.

"Yes, I will be a candidate for rehabilitation," Bundy said in court, "but not for what I have done, but what the system has done to me."

Bundy's attorney John D. O'Connell said he intends to file an appeal to the Utah State Supreme Court immediately.

Bundy's fate is now up to the Utah Board of Pardons which under ordinary circumstances might review a request for parole within six months of sentencing.

Judge Hanson reduced the charge from a first-degree to a second-degree count. A first-degree charge would have called for a sentence of 5 years to life.

Hanson said he reduced the charge because there were no other instances of criminal charges of a similar nature against Bundy.

Bundy appeared in Hanson's court as his own attorney for part of the proceedings and argued that his 90-day psychiatric evaluation at the Utah State Prison was inaccurate. Bundy objected to the psychiatric evaluation which described him as having an "antisocial personality," harboring "passive aggressiveness," being "a private person," "insecure," "hostile," and being unable to handle stress.

"He just underwent nine months of the worst stress I've seen, and he handled it better than Mr. Nixon handled Watergate, without breaking down," O'Connell said. Bundy also objected to the report's characterization of him as being "dependent on women."

"Who isn't dependent on women?" he asked the judge.

Bundy, who has spent the last 10 months in jail, told the judge before sentencing: "Someday, who knows when, 5 to 10 years in the future, when the time comes when I can leave, I suggest you ask yourself where we are, what's been accomplished, was the sacrifice of my life worth it all?"

— CHAPTER SIXTEEN —

September 1, 1976, exactly six months from the day of Ted's conviction, I was on my way to see him at the Utah State Prison. The day was hot and sunny, the kind of summer weather you can count on in Utah. The ninety-mile drive from Ogden to Draper gave me time to think.

It had been a battle to get to see Ted. The prison rule was that a single male prisoner could have only one unmarried female on his list of people cleared to visit, and Ted already had listed Kim Andrews. The prison officials told Ted that I could not visit him unless he took Kim's name off the list and put mine there in its place. As jealous as I was of Kim, I didn't want her to abandon him.

When I got to Utah, I called the warden's office and told the official I talked to how dumb I thought the rule was, but he justified it by saying that prison had a "romanticizing" effect on relationships that was bad for the prisoners. He told me that with the prison system as the adversary, couples were drawn tightly together. I thought that was ridiculous. "Look," I told him, "I've known Ted since 1969. I'm going to be in Utah for one week. If I lived here and wanted to see Ted every week, I could see your point. One week's worth of visits is not going to pit Ted and me together against your system." I was prepared to keep fighting until I got my way. After considerable discussion, he gave in.

I was perplexed by the anger that seemed to be always there, just beneath the surface. I had always thought of myself as sweet and nice, but now that I had stopped drinking, I seemed to boil with anger. I kidded myself about being even-tempered—mad all the time. But it was a real problem. My letters to Ted were full of complaints about the way Molly and I were getting along. She was the bright spot in my life but staying sober and carving out a new life an inch at a time left me exhausted and short-tempered.

The person who got most of my anger was Ted. I wrote him dreadful hot-and-cold letters that started out by telling him how much I missed him and loved him and then moved on to the same dead-end issue—his infidelity. I really did love him, but I wanted my revenge, too. In a way it was a relief to feel angry at somebody besides myself.

The prison was a huge concrete box baking in the sun off to the right of the freeway. Ted had told me that the temperature inside routinely got up to 102 degrees—just like his old apartment. But now he couldn't go out for a drink to cool off. After he was sentenced, Ted vowed that he would never accept and adapt to prison. His mood was grim, and he complained of insomnia and of feeling abandoned. He was angry at his mom who talked to him about faith, prayer, salvation, and destiny. He wrote me that he would not feel guilty for things he had not done.

I looked up at the guard tower. *This really is a prison,* I thought.

"You can't take your purse in," the guard in the lobby barked at me. Back to the car, lock the purse in the trunk. Back inside the prison lobby. "I need your driver's license," said the guard. Back to the car, get the license, back to the guard. "You can't take those keys in," he said. What was I supposed to do with the car keys, lock them in the car? I asked the guard if he could keep them for me in his little cubicle. He grudgingly agreed. As he filled out the record with my name, I saw Kim Andrews's name and birthdate, 1952. In 1952, I was teacher's pet in Miss Wilson's second-grade class. The guard told me I would be able to enter the visiting area in about ten minutes.

I took my place against a wall with the other families and friends. I nervously rolled the tassels from my Mexican blouse around my fingers, not wanting to look around. I didn't belong here.

The ten-minute wait seemed to last forever. Finally, everybody moved forward into a little holding room. The door by which we had entered was closed electrically and the door to the visiting room opened. The visitors and prisoners rushed towards each other. I wanted to scream.

At first, I couldn't see Ted. Then he grabbed my arm and pulled me to him and hugged me tight. He led me to some chairs in a corner and we sat down, facing each other, holding hands, our knees mixed up together. He looked so handsome. He had on jeans and a blue work shirt, and he had a tan—from the hours working out at the Draper Racquetball Club, as he put it. He looked just like he used to look when we went off to go rafting.

The room was noisy and there were little kids jumping around. *This is not real*, I kept telling myself. *This is not real; this is not Ted's life*. I couldn't speak. He stared at me.

"How was your drive?" he finally said. It was such a silly question that we both laughed. Then between the I-love-yous and the gee-you-look-greats, we talked nonstop. I told him about Molly; he told me about the friends he had made in prison. We talked about getting sober. He had been going to recovery meetings in prison because he was so excited about what I was going through. We talked about the "new me" and how proud he was of me. He asked me if I'd been dating.

"Oh, some," I answered, trying to sound nonchalant. I had gone to bed with the first guy I had gone out with. It had been a cold and calculated act. It had felt like revenge when I planned it, but it left me feeling hollow and shaken. It wasn't so easy for me to be irresponsible when I didn't have wine and beer to help. I had learned a lot from the experience, but now Ted was prying it out of me, and it made me angry—as if I were accountable to him for my actions. That led us to a polite argument about Kim, and Ted changed the subject.

We began talking about the poetry he had written for me. He was proud of it and I loved it, but I heard myself saying, "I really wanted to ask you not to write any more poetry to me. I find it just too upsetting. Sometimes I wonder if you send the same poems to other people."

The pain in his eyes made me wish I'd never said it. I didn't mean it—I only wanted to hurt him the way he hurt me.

"I write you those poems because I love you," he said.

I pulled my chair up to his so I could put my arms around him. I was sickened by my own anger and the pride that wouldn't let me back down. "I love you," I told him. "I'm sorry that I'm spoiling this time we have together."

We held each other for a little while, and with my anger out of the way, we could begin to talk more naturally. I asked him to give me a back-tickle.

"Not here," he said.

"Then where?" I asked him.

He felt foolish but he tickled my back for me. We kissed a lot, but it was very restrained. There was no point in getting turned on. We went back to conversation.

In the middle of talking about his family, he suddenly said flatly, "I can't live in here. Something's going to happen. Soon."

I was horrified. I knew he was talking about escape. His letters had hinted at it. "No," I told him. "It'll only cause more problems."

"Every day I'm in here. I'm dying," he said. "I can't live like this."

"Don't tell me about it," I said quickly.

We began talking about ordinary things again and soon it was time for me to leave. We both began crying hard. I promised to come back on Sunday before my plane left for Seattle. I wanted him to leave with me now.

I was herded into the holding area, but I could see the guards pat him down. He turned around and waved to me. Then he was gone. I collected my keys and stumbled out into the hot sunlight, and I thought the agony of leaving him would kill me. As I drove out of the parking lot, I saw a bunch of colorful hang gliders coming off the mountain on the other side of the freeway, flying free in sight of the prison.

If I ever needed a drink to take away reality, I needed one then, but I thought how disappointed Ted would be if I slipped.

When I came to the turnoff for Murray, I left the freeway and pulled into a gas station to get directions to the Fashion Place Mall. When Ted was out on bail, he had let me read a copy of the police report on Carol DaRonch's abduction. Now I wanted to retrace her steps.

I parked behind Sears, as she had, and walked through the store into the mall. The report had said something about the Walden bookstore. I stood in front of it. I tried to picture Ted approaching, wearing green slacks and patent leather shoes. No, it didn't compute. I leaned against the building and watched people walk by. There were several young, attractive women shopping by themselves. Would Ted see them as victims? Someone did. If a man came up to me right now and said he was a police officer, what would I do? Would I go with him? If he was as handsome and well-mannered as Ted, I might. The way the phony police officer had led Carol DaRonch all around the mall made me think that he enjoyed toying with his victim. *I shouldn't be doing this*, I thought. My face was flushed. I had the kind of headache you get from eating ice cream too fast. I found a phone book and looked up the address of the Salt Lake Recovery Club. These are places where recovering alcoholics can go for coffee and company. I wanted to be around something positive.

I pulled out of the north side of the mall's parking lot and headed east. I tried to find the school where the man had stopped and slammed the handcuffs on DaRonch. I could almost see her fighting off her attacker, and I could feel her fear. But I could not see what he looked like. This was stupid to be doing this to myself. I headed for the Recovery Club.

I talked to a woman at the club for a while, but it didn't help much. I was afraid to go back to my parents' house. I wasn't afraid of the Scotch they kept—it was the hunting rifles in the basement. It hadn't been hard for me to see that my drinking had been a slow form of suicide. Now when I flew into a self-destructive rage it wasn't drinking I thought about, but putting a gun in my mouth and blowing my head off.

I called Pat, my good friend in sobriety in Seattle. It was hard for me to ask for help. I told her that I'd been to the prison and that I was a little bit shaky. I was afraid that if I told her how crazy I really was, she wouldn't be my friend anymore. Talking with her gave me the strength to go back to Ogden, but I knew I didn't have the strength to go back to the prison to see Ted again.

I knew I should see Ted again because I had told him I would and he would be counting on it, but I couldn't. I called the prison and asked if they would give him a message. Absolutely not, I was told. I didn't know what else to do, so I sent him a mailgram telling him that I would not be there. I felt guilty about putting myself first, but guilty or not, I still wasn't going to go.

When I got back to Seattle there was a letter from Ted waiting for me:

Our two hours together was without doubt the most emotionally intense experience of my life. I wouldn't trade the experience for anything in the world, though, unless I was offered my freedom to be with you.

The next letter I had from him was an extremely painful one dated September 7, two days after the Sunday I didn't show up.

If I sound bitter it is because I am. This is not your problem any longer as you well recognize. Perhaps I am too much of a sentimentalist but as difficult as it would have been I would have liked to say goodbye to you in person, kiss you one last time. . . . Sunday, as I sat on the bench in the prison yard, basking in the sun, the fear grew with each hour. What a pathetic creature I must have appeared to be. Watching, waiting. Then three o'clock arrived and three fifteen and three thirty and three fifty and finally four. I waited until the bitter end. I imagined you driving to the airport and boarding the plane just a few miles away and I was struck with the panic of a caged animal. I felt the suicidal urge to run at the barbed wire fence and run and run to say goodbye to you before the plane flew you away from me forever. Crying, trembling as the last minutes ticked away I kept pleading softly to myself, "Please, Liz, please." Please don't leave me this way, I thought. Sunday was the most demoralizing day of my life. Sunday I think I finally recognized how powerless and weak I am.

Our letters continued. He tried to explain to me the pressures and expectations that build in a prisoner. I was embarrassed by my disregard for what he was going through. I tried to be more sensitive to his needs. Our letters flowed back and forth, and we wrote about how much we loved each other, but with less intensity than before my trip to Utah.

In October, a year after he had been arrested and charged with kidnapping, Ted was charged with first-degree murder in Colorado for the death of Caryn Campbell, who disappeared from a ski lodge near Aspen on January 12, 1975. In his letter to me Ted insisted on his innocence.

> This case they filed is based on information they have had since last February. . . . But it [the evidence] was manufactured. . . . The prosecution filed a witness list and on it are the names: Carol DaRonch, Jerry Thompson, David Yocum and Robert Keppel (King Co.). It is going to be like a rerun of a bad dream. DaRonch crying, Thompson lying ("Yes, I saw four pairs of patent leather shoes in his house") and Keppel implying ("He's pretty weird and a suspect in 4,900 disappearances."). It's an innuendo case. Dammit, I am not grandstanding, Liz. I am innocent and they are going to frame their little heads off. . . . Please try to believe in me.

I didn't know what to believe. I thought it possible that the police would plant evidence, but on the other hand, dammit, why was Ted in Colorado when he wasn't supposed to be? One of the main pieces of evidence the prosecutors had was the ski brochure Ted was carrying when he walked off the plane to visit me in January 1975. The police said there was a checkmark next to the name of a resort called the Wildwood Inn, the place from which Caryn Campbell was abducted.

Ted had told me that the man sitting next to him on the plane had given the brochure to him. If Ted had killed Caryn Campbell three days before he came to see me, would he be carrying such a telltale piece of evidence?

He wanted to know if I would come to Colorado for the trial. It wasn't easy to tell him that I wouldn't go through another trial. I asked him to understand. He sent me an anguished reply, a poem.

> *Into a raging river*
> *you and I were tossed.*
> *Separately, we are swept along,*
> *trying desperately to save ourselves.*
>
> *I understand survival.*
> *I practice it myself*
> *Neither of us has the strength*
> *to pull the other to the shore.*

A few days later Ted was sentenced to fifteen days in isolation, "the hole," for suspicion of attempting to escape. He told me what happened:

> *On Tuesday afternoon, I was searched, and a friend's social security card was found in my pocket. Later that afternoon, while I was resting in my cell on B block, several officers appeared and began searching my cell. With no further explanation, my things were packed and taken away and I was escorted to maximum security. . . . I would try to explain more of the story to you but I am not sure if these letters are read. It is sufficient to say that I never seriously planned or attempted to escape. . . . The situation*

is frightfully depressing and distressing, especially in light
of the fact that I had recently thoroughly adjusted myself
to making the best of prison life in hopes of being released
in the shortest period of time.

He described "the hole" as having a steel door, a small window, walls littered with graffiti, a urine and vomit stench, a concrete slab to sleep on, no commissary, no visits, and no companionship.

I hated more than anything else to be treated as if I was stupid. I fired a letter back to him.

It sounds like your current accommodations are a delight.
You got more bad press when your plans and current situa-
tion hit the front page of both papers. . . . But I guess what
really got me was your grandstanding to the omnipotent
authorities through your letter to me. The facts, to me,
show that you perhaps earned your way into the god-
forsaken Hole. It makes me sick to think of what you are
going through but I can't bleed for you. I get caught up in
a way of thinking that I can somehow influence what you
do or don't do. Or that if I suffer along with you, somehow
your suffering will be lessened. But it is too heavy a price
to pay. I know your need for support at this time is acute
but know that I only have a limited supply because I must
look out for myself first.

But in my next letter to him I was telling him that:

it was an immense relief to me to know you're o.k. That my
"blast" as you call it didn't blow you away. . . . Confusion
reigns Supreme. Just know that I love you.

159

Two steps forward and one step back.

We filled a need in each other—still. The letters flowed back and forth, amusing, comforting, understanding. But most of all, Ted's letters made me feel loved. I knew the words were only words, but they could still make me feel good. Right before Christmas he wrote me:

> No where in the hundreds of pages of letters I have written to you, I don't believe I ever successfully expressed the totality of what you, Elizabeth, are to me. Lord knows I have strained every brain cell to put your magic on paper. Every molecule in you, all the tones in your voice move me. My whole mind and body are gripped by your invisible power. The life I loved living is you. Laughter is you. Women are you. Sometimes I believe I am you. Memories, music, wind, rain, sleep are you. I am so lonely without life and life is you.

I had never spent Christmas anywhere but home in Utah, and this Christmas was to be no exception. Part of me didn't want to go to the prison to see Ted in a cage, but my heart said go. After the first of the year, he would be taken to Colorado to stand trial, and it would be harder to see him there. Once again I had to battle the warden's office; Kim Andrews was still the one woman on his visitors' list, and they didn't think exceptions should be made. But permission was finally granted and a time set up for my visit.

There wasn't much snow on the ground around the prison. It was a bright sunny day and I'd had my eyes dilated early that morning for my annual eye checkup. Even with my shades on, the sun was painful. As I pulled into the parking lot I thought about Gary Gilmore inside there somewhere. He had been sentenced to death, and he said that he looked forward to dying. I was appalled that Utah might be the first state to begin executing people again.

Ted was in maximum security after his escape attempt, and that was in a different building. I was much calmer checking in than I had been the last time, though my pupils felt like fifty-cent pieces and I wanted to tell the guard that I wasn't on drugs. But he, like everyone else I had dealt with at the prison, treated me as if I were some subnormal category of being, as if real people never went to prison and real people never came to visit them.

We had the visiting room all to ourselves. Ted was wearing what looked like white pajamas and he had a mustache. He looked great. The first topic of conversation was my hair. After wearing it long and straight forever, I'd had it cut long but really curly. We hung all over each other. When our hour was up, the guard shouted that it was time to go. Ted groaned and asked if we could have more time. To my surprise, the guard gave us another fifteen minutes. "There are some nice ones," Ted told me.

After much more than fifteen minutes, the guard said, "That's it."

"Five more minutes," Ted said. "We've got some crying to do." We had cried some as we talked—and laughed, too—and we cried when we said goodbye. It wasn't the gut-wrenching feeling that had gripped us last summer, but it was still hard. We walked with our arms around each other over to the gate back into "max." It still amazed me how well our bodies fit together. We embraced and kissed for so long I thought maybe the guard would come with orders to break it up. I turned and walked away. I didn't look back.

One morning in January, the first thing I heard when my clock radio came on was the news that Gary Gilmore had been executed by firing squad in Utah at the same prison where Ted was held. It was so real that I felt too sick to face the world another day. There had been a time when I didn't pay any attention to news of murders and criminals. Now I seemed to be affected by every murder I read about in the paper. I felt the horror of the victims, the anguish of their families, the sickness of the murderers, the disbelief of the criminals' families and friends. I despaired at what human beings do to other human beings.

At the end of January, Ted was moved to Colorado. He complained of the jail conditions, especially after he was moved to Glenwood Springs because the Aspen jail had been found unfit for long-term prisoners. The one good thing about Glenwood Springs was that he had access to a phone. He called me collect at least once a week, sometimes two or three times. I liked talking to him, but I felt weighted down by the calls. I knew the satisfying way we connected robbed me of the motivation to get out in the world and make some real friendships with people who were part of my day-to-day life.

March 1 was the anniversary of the date Ted was convicted. It seemed as if there had never been a time when he hadn't been in trouble.

In April, I celebrated my first year of sobriety with another day of profound depression. I burst into tears when called on to speak at my recovery group.

In May, on Mother's Day, my car was stolen from in front of my house. The next day the police found it on a school playground. That same afternoon I got a call from my high school sweetheart, Ben. When I went away to college I jilted him, not once but several times. I would call him up and ask him to come back and then drop him again. He was such a funny, kind, ambitious guy. The instant I heard his voice, I knew he had come to take me away from the chaos, back into the simple life of high school and 1962. He had married, he said, had kids, and was now divorced. He was in Seattle on business. We got together and had a fine time hashing over old times. We made tentative plans for me to visit him in San Francisco when Molly was visiting her dad in the summer. I was happy about the whole thing, pleased that when Ted called I was able to keep it from him. I talked to Ted so often and for so long that there wasn't anything he didn't know about my life. I didn't want him to know about Ben because then he would barrage me with letters about being in the arms of another, et cetera, and I wanted to be free to do whatever I liked.

Just about the time that Ben was due back in Seattle, Ted jumped out of a courtroom window in Aspen and escaped. He was recaptured after six days during which time I worried that he would contact me and ask for help. Knowing that I would have no choice but to turn him in, I prayed that he would never put me in that position.

Back in prison, he called a few days later. He didn't want to talk about the escape other than to joke about falling out of a window and wandering around senseless in the Rocky Mountains. I told him as gently as I could that I was involved with someone. I didn't want him to hurt, but I wanted to go my own way. He wrote to me:

> *While I cannot now or ever be able to fully comprehend or accept the reality of you loving, touching, laughing with and caring for another man, I know now that such an inevitability must be dealt with on the kind of understanding level which knows your happiness is my ultimate concern. So I understand.*

Shortly after that, Ben told me I had too many problems for him, and he dropped me.

Ted continued to call, and as usual, it was Ted I turned to for understanding and support when I hurt. I told him that the "someone" was my high school boyfriend and he laughed. He told me more about what happened when he looked up his old flame, Susan Phillips.

> *Old lovers are too often vehicles to the serene, uncomplicated long ago dream world of lost youth, and like old used cars, old lovers too often have too many miles on them to make the trip back.*

I bought a new house, got a promotion at work, and no longer hated myself every minute of every day.

After I moved into my new house, Angie came for a visit. She had moved back to Utah. She had been going through some rough times herself, and as we talked we realized how much we meant to each other. We carefully avoided any mention of Ted, but we fell into a long conversation about life and what it was all about. I was able to share with her the things I had learned in recovery, but my pride wouldn't let me tell her where these ideas came from or that I was going to meetings to stay sober.

One of the steps to sobriety is making amends to those you have hurt. For a long time, I foolishly denied that I needed to make amends to anyone. The only person I had hurt with my drinking was myself. But being face to face with Angie and telling her I was sorry for the way things worked out was a tremendous relief. When she went back to Ogden, we ran up big phone bills getting to know each other again.

Since Ted had been in prison, we had developed a share-the-book program, where we read the same book at the same time and shared our views and ideas. We were reading *Shogun*, a love story. In one letter Ted quoted a passage describing the hero after his lover had been killed.

"Many times Blackthorne had looked over his shoulder expecting her to be there, but she was never there and never would be and this did not disturb him. She was with him forever, and he knew he would love her in the good times and the tragic times, even in the winter of his life. She was always on the edge of his dreams. And now those dreams were good, very good. . . ."

And he added his own words:

I feel you there, looking over my shoulder, a very powerful force in my life. Even though it is winter in my life, I still need you; I still love you.

I felt the same way about him; he was always there, looking over my shoulder. I didn't want to stop loving him or erase the power of his love from my life, but I needed real "in-the-flesh" relationships. So, it was back to therapy.

The therapist gave me a questionnaire to fill out and another one to give to a person who knew me well. I sent it to Ted. After I turned them in to be scored, the therapist told me I had scored in the ninety-eighth percentile, meaning that if I was in a room with a hundred people, there would be only one person in the room who was more depressed than me.

One day Ted called me at work and was talking about a friend who had been to see him. I asked him who the friend was, and he hemmed and hawed and then told me it was some guy he had met in Salt Lake City, but I knew he was lying. A woman named Carole Boone had been to see him. I didn't know who she was, and I didn't care.

He wrote me a long mournful letter.

I was shocked to be confronted with my old self today, my old petty, deceiving self. I was embarrassed, too. . . . It is a humiliating experience to be confronted with a weakness I thought I had corrected. It is a frightening thought to think that I am unable to correct it.

He wrote about death:

I am not sure I have the courage for that yet. My instinct to survive is strong, although that instinct seems so pathetic and pointless right now. What for? Who for? I bring pain to you; I bring pain to others who care for me and I bring pain to myself. It is time to rethink this awful experience because the stimulus of standing alone in the face of great odds is not satisfying anymore. It is time to re-evaluate the value of living without being alive. . . . The crazy flow of things seems to have stopped. I want to look around me now. I want to master life and death.

Shortly before Christmas, Ted's motion for a change of venue was granted. The trial would be held in Colorado Springs—the prosecutor's hometown and probably the most conservative place in Colorado. Juries there routinely sentenced people to death. Ted was beside himself. Shortly after this, Colorado's death penalty was found to be unconstitutional, so that burden was off his mind. He still couldn't believe that he was to be tried in Colorado Springs. The prosecutor, Milton Blakely, had been loaned to Aspen to prosecute Ted, and now a judge had moved the trial back to Blakely's hometown.

Before I left to go to Utah for Christmas, I got a letter from Ted saying there could be no goodbyes, and that whatever happened he wanted to make sure that I knew he loved me and that my memory was with him always. It was the same kind of letter he had been sending me for the past year and a half, and I was resigned to the fact that our relationship would never end. While I was in Utah, he called me at my parents' house. "It just makes more trouble for me," I complained.

He explained that he only wanted to hear my voice one more time.

"How many times have we gone through this?" I laughed.

He wasn't laughing. He was dead serious.

I was back in Seattle on the afternoon of New Year's Eve when Detective Keppel called about one o'clock. "Ted's gone," he said. "He's got an eight-hour jump. No one knows where he is."

CHAPTER SEVENTEEN

Ted had told me after his first escape in Colorado that he had no regrets about trying to gain his freedom, and that he would do it again if the opportunity arose. According to Keppel, Ted had crawled through a hole in the ceiling of his cell, sometime during the night, and no one had noticed he was gone until noon.

"If you hear anything," Keppel said, "call me immediately."

I had made plans to spend New Year's Eve with some girlfriends, and we went out to dinner. Molly was spending the night with one of her friends. When I got home at one in the morning I halfway expected to find Ted in my house. I was a lot more jittery than the last time he'd escaped. I told myself that it was because I was afraid he might seek help from me, but as I lay awake that night, listening to every creak in my new house, I admitted to myself that I might be afraid of Ted. I pushed the thought out of my mind. Ted loved me. He wasn't capable of murder. I decided I was scared because I felt so vulnerable in this house. In my old place, there were always people around and all the windows were high up off the ground. The next day I nailed my basement windows shut.

I knew I was overreacting, but my mind kept going back to a phone conversation Ted and I had several months earlier. He told me that some young female hitchhikers had been brought into the jail at Glenwood Springs, and that he could see them from the room where he'd been watching TV. He talked generally about how long it had been since he'd had sex, but his conversation was disoriented, and he seemed kind of weird. It had given me shivers at the time because he hadn't sounded like the ever-in-control Ted I knew. A letter I received from him in November had bothered me immensely. He was responding to my complaint that I was afraid to establish relationships with people, and he wrote:

> You see yourself withdrawing from people, afraid to estab-
> lish friendships, loveships (?). I have known people who,
> without saying a word, radiate vulnerability. Their facial
> expressions say "I am afraid of you." These people invite
> abuse. I don't know why but they do. Is it their self-concept?
> By expecting to be hurt do they subtly encourage it? And if
> some mental switch could be thrown and tomorrow they
> expected to be happy and excited with each person they
> met, could that happen, too?

I didn't want to fall into the bag that the press and the police were in. They assumed that Ted was a murderer, so everything he said had some weird double meaning to it. But I wished he hadn't written that.

On Sunday night there was a news report that Ted had been sighted in Tacoma. I doubted it very much, but as the evening wore on I decided that Ted had to be somewhere, and it could very well be Tacoma. I felt like a fool, but I called the King County Police dispatcher and asked him to call Keppel at home for me. After all I had been through with the King County Police, it wasn't easy to swallow my pride and ask them for help. As it turned out, Keppel couldn't be reached, but I talked to the dispatcher for a long time. We agreed that Ted would be crazy to come to the Northwest where his face was so well known. He arranged for the Seattle Police to cruise my neighborhood frequently, and he sent a plainclothes officer over to talk with me. He told me that if I was in trouble, I should open the blinds on the front window as a signal.

As the days passed, my fear subsided. Molly and I talked about all the possibilities and what she should do if any of them occurred. I had to keep reminding myself that Ted loved us and would not hurt us. The first time he escaped, I was secretly happy that he was free, but this time I was frightened. I continued to deny to myself that he was a dangerous person, but that didn't match up with my gut feeling. At a recovery meeting I met Hank, a man who was handsome, big, and strong. Although we didn't have a lot in common other than our recovery from alcoholism, he made me feel safe. He began to stay with me even at night.

One day at work I got a call from the prosecutor in Colorado. He wondered if I would be willing to talk with him about what Ted had told me of his upcoming trial. In other words, he wanted to know what I could tell him about Ted's defense strategy. I thought this was a new low.

Soon the FBI men started coming around during work. I had recently moved into a new office after my department merged with another one. The people I had worked with over the years knew who these good-looking men in three-piece suits were and why they were there, but it puzzled the people I had just gotten to know. Feeling like a sideshow freak, I explained about me and Ted Bundy.

The FBI had entered the search for Ted on the theory that he had fled across state lines. The agent I dealt with must have spent years perfecting his mechanical I-am-the-law manner. He wanted to know about the last time I'd talked with Ted and the last time I'd seen him. Did I ever send him cash? (No.) Did I know he was planning to escape? (No.) Did I know where he was? (No.) He warned me that if I helped Ted or knew where he was and didn't tell them, I would be guilty of aiding and abetting and would go to prison for it. He didn't need to tell me that. I may have been screwed up but I wasn't stupid.

I said something to the agent about not understanding why my life continued to be so chaotic.

"Maybe it's the company you keep," he said.

He wanted to know if he could talk with Molly. I thought that was an odd request. She didn't know where Ted was, but if he thought it would do some good he was welcome to talk with her. He came to our house and asked me to leave the room. Later Molly said that he asked her how she felt about Ted and if he ever touched her body or talked dirty to her. *What does that have to do with finding Ted?* I wondered. He asked me if he could see the last letter Ted had sent me. Ted had, for the past few months, been sending me *Cathy* comic strips that he clipped from the newspaper. He said Cathy reminded him of me. She had this self-centered, egomaniac boyfriend named Irving that Ted said was his Siamese twin. This last letter from Ted had several *Cathy* strips enclosed, and Ted had signed it "Irving."

The FBI agent pounced on the signature. "Does he go by Irving very often?"

I tried to explain that he never went by the name Irving, that it was a joke, but I saw "Irving" go down in the FBI report as an a/k/a (also known as).

One morning in mid-January I picked up the newspaper and saw a picture of a frightened woman peering out of a gap in the drawn drapes of her sorority house. The story said an intruder had raped and murdered two young women and beaten two others as they slept in their beds at Florida State University in Tallahassee. I previously told the FBI agent that I thought Ted would be found on a university campus somewhere. Now I had the ominous feeling that he was in Tallahassee, the same kind of feeling I'd had when I was handed the composite picture that started all my worries back in 1974.

The agent was scheduled to see me that day, but he didn't put much stock in my fear that Ted was in Florida. Instead he wanted to know what kind of shoes Ted was fond of, what kind of cars he liked, what kind of music, and what kind of food. The FBI was about to put Ted on their "Ten Most Wanted" list. When I was growing up I got hooked on radio shows—*Boston Blackie* and others that closed with the line, "If you see anyone matching this description, contact your nearest law enforcement agency immediately." Now it was happening in real life.

Later that day my mom called me from Utah to tell me that an FBI man had been to see her. She had told him to look for Ted in Florida because of a picture she had seen in the paper that morning. Much later, Keppel told me that he called Florida as soon as he saw the picture of the sorority girl, and told the police to look for Ted Bundy.

Keppel asked me if they could put a "trap" on my phone. A trap differs from a tap in that a trap only tells where calls are coming from, but you can't listen to the conversation. I thought that Ted would call me sooner or later, so I agreed. In a way, that relieved some of the responsibility for turning him in. The phone company called to discuss the procedure, but the trap had not yet been installed when Ted called me on Thursday, February 16, 1978.

I had just got home from work about five o'clock and was putting my bike away, when a thoroughly shaken Molly told me that Ted was on the phone. "I didn't know what else to do," she told me, "so I accepted the charges."

"You shouldn't be calling me," I told him. "There's a trap on the phone," I lied.

He was crying. "It's okay, it's okay. I'm in custody. It's all over."

"Where?" I asked.

"Well, I made a deal with the police. They aren't going to announce my arrest until tomorrow morning so that I can talk with you and my family. It's going to be bad when it breaks."

"I'm not going to call up Channel 7," I told him. "Where are you?"

"Florida—Pensacola."

"Oh, no! I was hoping you'd be picked up anywhere but Florida. I saw this picture in the paper last month—those sorority women were murdered. I told the FBI that I hoped you weren't there."

"It's going to be bad," he said, "really bad when it breaks tomorrow. I want you to be prepared. It could be really ugly."

"Are you a suspect in those murders?" I asked.

"I wish we could sit down . . . alone . . . and talk about things . . . with nobody listening . . . about why I am the way I am."

There was a long pause. I didn't want to know but I asked anyway. "Are you telling me . . . that you're sick?"

"Back off!" he barked. "I meant how come I've hurt you so many times."

I was startled by the abruptness of his answer. I said nothing.

"I wanted to call you on Valentine's Day," he said, "but I didn't quite make it." Still I said nothing.

"How's your love life?" he asked. "Anyone new in your life?" I told him that yes, I had fallen in love.

"He's a lucky guy," Ted told me. Soon we were talking as freely as we ever had. My friend Hank came into the bedroom where I was and demanded that I get off the phone. Molly had told him that I was talking to Ted. I shook my head, no. Hank stormed out and I soon heard his truck roar away. Ted and I kept talking.

I asked him about his escape from Colorado, but he wouldn't talk about it. He did talk about his first days of freedom and about sitting in a bar in Michigan and watching the University of Washington Huskies play Michigan in the Rose Bowl. I tried to remember how afraid I had been when he escaped, but it seemed unreasonable now. Soon I heard Hank returning. Ted asked if he could talk with Hank for a minute. Hank looked so agitated that I thought he might throw up, but he was answering "I know" and "I will" to Ted's exhortations to take good care of me and Molly.

"May God have mercy on your soul," Hank said and gave the phone back to me.

Ted and I continued to talk. I told him I was surprised that he was back in custody, that I thought he would rather be dead than be a prisoner again.

"I thought so, too," he told me. "I'm really disappointed in myself. I just didn't have what it takes to die."

I wanted to talk more about the circumstances of his arrest, particularly about the murders I'd read about. He told me not to bring it up again, that he didn't want to talk about it.

"But why are the police waiting till tomorrow to make this public?" I asked. "What was your end of the bargain?"

"They didn't know who they had," he told me. "I've been playing with them since Wednesday. I finally told them who I was in exchange for these phone calls."

We talked for close to an hour and then he told me he had better call his mother. He asked me if he could call me back later, and I told him yes, he could. I would accept the charges.

I lay on my bed exhausted. Molly and Hank wanted to know what he'd said. When I came to the part about calling me back later, they both told me I shouldn't talk to him again. I knew they were probably right, but I just felt so bad for him.

About an hour later the phone rang again, but this time Hank answered it. Although we had agreed on what he would say, I thought I would pass out when I heard him say, "No, operator, we won't accept charges."

I called the FBI and asked them to have Dale Kelly, the agent who had interviewed me, call me back. I wanted to know if Ted was a suspect in the murders I'd read about. Kelly had told me repeatedly to call him if Ted contacted me. I was sure, though, since Ted was in custody, that the FBI was aware of it. I was surprised that at seven o'clock Dale Kelly was still at work. I was even more surprised that Kelly didn't believe me when I said I had talked to Ted and that he was in custody.

"Where?" he demanded. "How do you know it was Ted? Could it have been an impostor?"

Even after I told him that it was Ted, no doubt in my mind, one hundred percent sure, he continued to ask me, "Are you sure?" He never did answer my question about the Florida State murders.

At 2:00 A.M. the next Saturday, the phone rang. I was out of bed and into the living room before I was even awake. It was a collect call from Ted.

"I want to talk about . . . what we were talking about on Thursday," he said, haltingly.

"About being sick?" I asked.

"Yes. . . . I've been talking with a priest." He was crying. "I'm going to try to clear things up in a way . . . that I'll be back in Washington. I have a . . . responsibility . . . to those who have suffered, and I want to reconcile things," he went on in a weak voice.

"I love you," I said. "I just don't know what to say." Hank had come into the living room and was motioning me to get off the phone. I shot him my fiercest go-to-hell look. I signaled to him to get me a pencil and paper. I knew that I wouldn't remember what Ted was telling me if I didn't write it down.

"I was afraid you would have nothing to do with me if I told you." His voice was so weary that I started to cry. "Didn't you . . . always think it was possible?"

"No," I said. "I didn't think it could be true. I had my doubts. but . . . I just couldn't accept it. Sometimes . . . I wondered if it was me . . . that you hated me . . . and wanted to kill me."

"No. There is something the matter with me. It wasn't you. It was me. I just couldn't contain it. I've fought it for a long, long time . . . it got too strong. We just happened to be going together when it got under way. I tried, believe me, I tried to suppress it. It was taking more and more of my time. That's why I didn't do well in school. My time was being used trying to make my life look normal. But it wasn't normal. All the time I could feel that force building in me. . . ." His voice faded off for a moment. "You can ask me questions, if you want. I'll try to answer the best I can."

I felt a million years old. I wished I could hold him in my arms and rock him back and forth. "What about the Florida murders? . . . Are you going to be charged with those?"

"Oh, Liz. I can't talk about Tallahassee, but anything else I'll try to answer."

"Did you ever . . ." How was I going to put this? "Did you ever want . . . to kill me?"

There was a long, heavy silence. "Well, there was one time when I was really trying hard to control it, so I'd been staying off the streets and trying to feel normal. But it just happened that I was sleeping with you at your house when I felt it coming on. I closed the damper so the smoke couldn't go up the chimney, and then I left and put a towel in the crack under the door so the smoke would stay in the apartment."

I remembered that night well. I'd been pretty drunk by the time we climbed into the hide-a-bed in front of the fireplace. I woke up briefly as Ted was leaving, and he told me he was going back to his house to get his fan because the fireplace was backed up. I had sleepily pulled the covers over my head because I couldn't breathe. But soon I couldn't breathe under the covers, either. My eyes were running, and I was coughing. I jumped out of bed and threw open the nearest window and stuck my head out. After I had recovered some, I opened all the windows and the doors and broke up the fire the best I could. I had gotten on Ted the next day for not coming back with the fan. As he told me now that he had wanted me to die that night, I almost didn't believe him. It didn't fit in with the murders. I thought that maybe he wasn't willing to talk about any more serious attempts to kill me.

I told him that I sometimes wondered if he used me to touch base with reality, like the night Carol DaRonch was kidnapped and Debbie Kent vanished, and he called me at midnight. Or taking me out for hamburgers after what happened at Lake Sammamish.

"Yeah, that's a pretty good guess," he said. "It's like it's over. I don't have a split personality. I don't have blackouts. I remember everything I've done. Like Lake Sammamish. We went out to Farrell's for ice cream after eating hamburgers. It wasn't like I had forgotten or couldn't remember, but it was just over . . . gone . . . the force wasn't pushing me anymore. I don't understand it. The force would just consume me. Like one night, I was walking by the campus and I followed this sorority girl. I didn't want to follow her. I didn't do anything but follow her and that's how it was. I'd be out late at night and follow people like that. . . . I'd try not to, but I'd do it anyway."

"What about Brenda Ball? I remember you took my family and me out for pizza that night and then hurried away only to be late for Molly's baptism the next day. Is that where you were?"

He mumbled something that I couldn't understand and then said, "It's pretty scary, isn't it?"

"But the police are saying that the murders started in 1969—that's the year we met. What was it that made it start in '69?"

"The police are years off," he told me.

"I thought if you ever got free, you'd never so much as jaywalk to stay free . . . and now this in Florida," I said.

"I know. Me, too. I loved my freedom. But I have a sickness . . .

a disease like your alcoholism . . . you can't take another drink and with my . . . sickness . . . there is something . . . that I just can't be around . . . and I know it now."

I asked him what that was, and he said, "Don't make me say it."

Throughout the conversation he kept telling me that I never needed to worry about Molly or myself. He talked of his responsibility to society and again, of arranging things so that he would be back in Washington State. I told him that I wouldn't be able to visit him in prison except once or twice. He said he wished things were different. I told him I thought he was doing the right thing and that I would pray for him, and we hung up.

I sat on the living room floor huddled in the afghan that Mom made for me. I stared at the floor while scenes of the good times and of the bad times played in my mind like a desolate slide show. I had prayed for so long "to know," and now the answer killed a part of me. I didn't learn until later that Ted would be charged with murdering Kimberly Leach, a twelve-year-old girl, the same age as Molly. I thought of Ted's assurances that I never needed to worry about me or Molly. I didn't understand Ted Bundy and I never will.

— CHAPTER EIGHTEEN —

Mount St. Helens erupted in 1980. And one picture of the destruction it caused stays in my mind. Most of the trees had been blown over and burned clean by the blast; the few that remained standing had no branches. The ground was covered with gray ash and mud. The sky matched the ground.

I looked at that bleak, desolate scene and thought, "That looks like I felt when I finally knew that Ted was a murderer." How could anyone believe that these things could happen?

The fury of the eruption of this beautiful mountain had destroyed everything in its path. The fury of whatever plagued Ted has destroyed a beautiful man and taken many, many lives with it. I say "whatever" because I am uncomfortable discussing the evil power that I know exists. I don't like to talk about it, partly because I don't want to sound like a fanatic, but mostly because it has come too close to mangling my life. I don't pretend to understand or accept Ted's compulsion to kill beautiful, vital young women. But I do understand something of compulsion, and I do understand something of what it feels like to repeat compulsive actions over and over again, even though the intention is never to do it again. In my case it was getting drunk repeatedly when I didn't want to. In Ted's case it was so much worse.

At times I felt as if I was engaged in hand-to-hand combat with an evil spirit over my sanity, my sobriety, and my soul. Even after years without a drink I find myself thinking how great one glass of white wine would taste. I know where one glass of wine would lead, and I know where these thoughts come from. My spiritual growth is extremely important to me now. I try to live my life according to

God's will. There is comfort in knowing that if I stay sober, the worst is behind me. I have always prayed a lot and still do. I pray for Ted, but I am sickened by him.

I was distraught as the days and then weeks flew by after his last middle-of-the-night phone call. He said he was going to make things right, but nothing happened. Why did he tell me the truth and then not act on it? I felt as if he had laid a burden on me.

The first thing in the morning after his call I phoned his Seattle attorney. I wanted him to know what Ted was trying to do. I wanted him to tell me what I should do with the information Ted had given me. He was sympathetic, but as Ted's attorney, he couldn't advise me. He gave me the name of another attorney, who suggested I go to the King County Police. I had to wait through a three-day weekend, but on the following Tuesday I gave a statement about the phone conversation to Detective Keppel and Captain Mackie.

When I told them that Ted had agreed to answer any of my questions and that I had asked him things like "What did I have to do with what happened?" Keppel was beside himself.

"Why didn't you ask him what happened to Jan Ott's bicycle? Or where Debbie Kent is?" he wanted to know.

Because I'm not a policeman, I thought. I had asked Ted the things I did for my own peace of mind. I needed to be sure that nothing I had done had triggered Ted's rampages.

I didn't hear from Ted until May, when he called me at work one day. He told me that his horoscope said it would be a day for jealousy, so he thought he would call me. The conversation was extremely strained. He wanted to know if I was getting married. He told me that he kept busy typing and reading and that his mental state was great most of the time. Sometimes he felt pretty grim, he said, but he didn't want to talk about that. His sister was getting married and he talked about his family. It would have been so easy to fall into the same comfortable conversations that we used to have, but I managed to force myself to tell him that I was surprised that he had done nothing about making things right as he had said he would do. He said that I would have to understand that it had been a very emotional time for him, and that in the light of new developments it was an inopportune time for such action.

In other words, he hadn't meant to tell me the truth, but it had slipped out under the stress of his recapture.

His talk of "new developments" disgusted me. What new developments could change the truth? I thought that he knew the game was over and that everyone else knew it, too. He certainly knew I wouldn't be standing behind him anymore. Tired and alone in Florida, his only hope had been to get back to Washington near his family. I didn't know what had changed. I suspected that someone, maybe Carole Boone, the woman he later married during his murder trial, was willing to stand behind him.

As our phone call ended, he told me he would try to call again. I told him not to, that Hank wouldn't like it. I still wasn't strong enough to tell him that I, Liz Kendall, did not want him in my life anymore.

At the end of June, I got a strange letter from him. It was addressed to me but had been sent to Carole Boone who forwarded it to me with an odd, light-hearted cover letter. Ted wrote that he had heard I had gone to the police and had been saying some "fairly uncomplimentary things" about him. He said he was having a hard time believing I would do something like that.

> From a purely factual perspective, the reports filtering back to me reveal what you allegedly told these people and what I told to you over the phone that night from Pensacola are two very different accounts. . . . I still can-

not imagine you broadcasting the conversation we had. While I will not pretend to be Prince Charming, I do think it fair to say that for 2 1/2 years now I have done everything to keep your name out of the news and avoid embarrassment for you. . . . Several friends and reporters have called me a fool since they believe that you were in some way responsible for the things that were happening to me. . . . But if you did go to the police, you went to them thinking they might be able to use what you thought you had heard. What if, dear Elizabeth, the King County authorities were desperate enough to charge me, based on your representations. . . . Do you want to hurt me so badly that you would twist the truth to see me swing from some wooden beam by my neck? . . . All I am saying is that you could have gotten yourself in much hot water, and you are fortunate that what you thought you had was of no value to the police. . . . If you did what I have been told you did, you were not thinking of your welfare, or Molly's, or your parents' or your new life.

As sickened as I was by the letter, the guilt trip didn't work anymore; it didn't change the truth. Several weeks later he called and sheepishly told me that he had never intended to mail the letter and that he was very sorry that he had ever written it. We talked for less than a minute. It was the shortest phone conversation we had ever had, and it was also the last time I talked to him.

Ted's problems continue to affect me in many ways. On one level I find I have developed a grim view of human beings and what they are capable of doing to other human beings. That makes it hard for me to get very close to people. On an outer level, I have to deal with writers and reporters and private investigators who barge into my life.

Unfortunately, I read everything that is written about Ted. One recent magazine article said:

> This speculation in the press, filtering back to Seattle, resulted in the police getting their first real tip on Ted Bundy as a possible suspect. Ironically, it came from his Seattle girlfriend, whose suspicions had been stirred in a fit of jealous anger and vengeance over the feeling that Bundy was being unfaithful to her and was trying to end their relationship.

Yes, I was jealous of Ted. I loved him and wanted to be his wife, but I did not call the police because I was jealous.

I've thought a lot about the jealous feelings I had about Ted. I was so insecure when I met him, my self-esteem rocked by a series of setbacks going back to my freshman year in college—the same time when I began discovering the pleasures of alcohol. I hated, hated, hated being divorced. I wanted a stable, loving home for my daughter and the other kids who would come along. I handed Ted my life and said, "Here, take care of me." He did in a lot of ways, but I became more and more dependent upon him. When I felt his love, I was on top of the world; when I felt nothing from Ted, I felt that I was nothing. But the fuel that fed my jealousy was his inconsistent treatment of me. We would be getting along fine and then a door would slam and I would be out in the cold until Ted was ready to let me back in. I'd spend hours trying to figure out what I had done or said that was wrong. And then, suddenly, he would be warm and loving again and I would feel needed and cared for.

In that middle-of-the-night phone call from Florida, Ted told me that he tried to stay away from me when he felt the power of his sickness building in him. I wondered if those times coincided with the times I felt so left out, felt that he was hiding something from me. I suspected that it was other women, and it often was, but he was also hiding a terrible secret. He loved life and enjoyed it to the fullest. The tragedy is that this warm and loving man is driven to kill.

As I reread *The Phantom Prince* in preparation for the publication of the updated edition, I realized how much I have changed over the years. There are pages I felt like ripping out because they made me so uncomfortable. The most cringeworthy line is on the last page: "The tragedy is that this warm and loving man is driven to kill." The second-most cringeworthy thing I wrote is on the first page of the original preface. I said, "I have come to accept that a part of me will always love a part of him."

I do have compassion for the me who wrote those things so many years ago. Although I was sober and getting counseling at the time I wrote the book, I was still in denial. Even after I had heard it from Ted himself that, yes, he was a serial killer, I stayed in a confused state for some time. I was constantly running scenarios in my head, trying to make sense of Ted and Liz and what had happened. The experience of our relationship seemed so real, and the things I learned about his brutal attacks seemed completely surreal. My counselor told me that obsessive-compulsive disorder often develops in people who have experienced trauma. She was the first to point out that my obsessive mental review of "Ted and Liz" was part of my denial. I know now that I was trying to protect myself from the unfathomable truth.

By writing in the book that Ted was warm and loving and lovable, I was avoiding facing the painful truth that I knew only a small part of Ted. And that small part was rapidly being overtaken by the rageful sexual deviant in him, as he repeatedly acted out his murderous fantasies.

In the years since the book was published, I've worked on knowing and accepting the totality of Ted. It's been harder than hell. In the beginning, if I let my guard down for a minute, I'd recall the Ted who I thought I loved and had fun with. My mind could run with that endlessly—he was smart, he made me laugh, our chemistry was good, and on and on. I would have to go through the brutal litany of facts about what he did to remember the truth.

A few of the horrendous facts include: He abducted and killed two women in one day and then took me out to dinner that evening. He raped and murdered women and then slept with me. He took my visiting family out for a fun evening of pizza. He then excused himself, went to a bar in South Seattle, found a young woman, and murdered her. The next day he was his charming self at a family event. One day when he was driving to Utah to go to law school, he called from Nampa, Idaho, to tell me he loved me. I learned later that he abducted a young woman that day and murdered her. He caused so much heartbreak and worry for the families and friends of women who went missing without a trace, and he didn't care. For those who knew their loved one was murdered, he left them trying not to think about last moments. As I write this, the facts are so unspeakably awful; I don't know why it took me so long to accept the truth, but it did.

Now is a good time to clarify something. When I say it was harder than hell for me to face the facts, I know that my version of "hard" is nothing compared to how hard it must be for those who have had to grieve the loss of someone they love, someone who is no longer alive because of Ted Bundy. I am grateful that my daughter and I survived him. It is a gift to be able to make mistakes, find solutions, and move forward in life—a gift not to be wasted.

This is my chance to write a more clear-eyed version of the statements that I wrote so many years ago. "The tragedy is that this warm and loving man is driven to kill" should read, "The tragedy is that this violent and manipulative man directed his murderous rage at innocent young women to satisfy his insane urges." And now that he is dead, I would add, "Compounding the tragedy, he only told the truth—and then only partly—when he thought it was a bargaining chip to prolong his life." In my rewrite, the sentence "I have come to accept that a part of me will always love a part of him" would need to be completely deleted. Period.

The Phantom Prince seemed a perfect title for my book. I thought I had found my prince, especially in the first few years we were together. I was so enthralled and happy with my handsome Ted that I was willing to toss my own values aside and accept that he lied sometimes, and he stole a few things. There were so many things about him that were perfect in my eyes that I was blindly in love. But, of course, he wasn't who I imagined him to be. Ted, himself, summed it up when he wrote a poem for me while in prison. He described combing back my hair, moving his hands on my back, and his lips caressing my ear—all the things I once loved.

The last verse included these lines, which still haunt me:

> *when we moved together loving,*
> *did we need the world's permission?*
> *when we later lay unmoving*
> *had you loved*
> *an apparition?*

My answer: yes, most definitely.

The day Ted was executed was an emotionally blank day for me. By the time I woke up in Seattle at eight o'clock on the morning of Tuesday, January 24, 1989, Ted was already dead in Florida. The electric chair had done its grisly job of killing a gruesome man. I don't remember anything I did that day. I've never believed in capital punishment, but I hoped Ted's death brought closure to the people who loved the women he killed and to those women who survived.

There had been other execution dates set in the ten years since Ted was sentenced to death for murdering Margaret Bowman and Lisa Levy as they slept in their sorority house, and twelve-year-old Kimberly Leach, who was the same age as Molly was at the time.

Ted and I had very little contact after his middle-of-the-night phone call in February 1978, right after he was arrested in Florida. In that call, he confessed without being specific about his acts. He told me he was sick and there was a force in him that he couldn't control. He said he was going to confess the things he had done and the people he had hurt. When he didn't, I was mad. He started proclaiming his innocence in the media again. I knew the truth and was disgusted. Nevertheless, in 1986, when it seemed his execution was imminent, I felt compelled to write him a goodbye note, in which I briefly told him the reasons I fell in love with him when we first met. Just hours before his execution, the US Court of Appeals issued a stay. He lived another few years, but I never contacted him again.

One of the questions I am asked often is whether I think Ted loved me and Molly. Yes, I do. But who knows? I know I loved him, at least the part that he showed to me. It has been suggested that he needed a normal-looking life to hide his dark side, and that this was what we were to him. That could be true, too. We will never know.

Another thing that people want to know is how I could stay in the relationship after having my doubts and contacting law enforcement. The answer is that I was an emotional mess, I thought and hoped I was wrong, and I loved him. This choice has been hard for me to comprehend and accept, so I understand why people find it strange.

I do know the decisions I made allowed my daughter and me to survive Ted Bundy. A couple of years ago, I started wondering what would have happened if I had rejected Ted when he showed up at my Seattle door after he was bailed out of jail in Salt Lake City. My counselor at the time had recommended I stop interacting with Ted and the detectives, so I could focus on myself and my daughter. I had already told Detective McChesney I could not help law enforcement any longer. If I had told Ted to go away and leave us alone that day, would he have accepted that? Or would it trigger the explosive rage that we now know was in him?

REBUILDING MY LIFE

After Ted's conviction in Utah for attempted kidnapping in 1976, I contemplated moving. There were too many reminders in Seattle of my life with Ted. The only other place I wanted to live was Utah, to be close to my family. The stigma of being Ted's girlfriend would be just as bad there.

My job at the university was gratifying, and I liked and appreciated the men I worked with. I had started there as a secretary, the only woman in a small department with a dozen guys. When the department started growing rapidly, I took on more responsibilities and was promoted. I found it comforting that my coworkers had been there from the beginning of my relationship with Ted. Since he hung out at my office a lot and went to work functions with me, my coworkers knew that the man I fell in love with was different from the guy who was all over the news. They were supportive when everything blew up. This stability, when I felt like I was falling apart, was something I sorely needed. Much later, I learned they all thought Ted was guilty as hell and wished I would come to my senses.

Another reason I didn't want to move was that I was seriously depressed, and making a decision requiring action of any type was completely overwhelming. You would know from reading the original text that I was bottoming out in my alcoholism and that I started a sobriety program a month and a half after the Utah conviction. The thought of starting over with recovery work in a new city was exhausting. Thankfully I am still sober decades later.

By the time *The Phantom Prince* was published, I had already married and divorced Hank. The only good thing I can say about the marriage is that having a husband helped me not get sucked back into the quagmire of my past. I could tell Ted not to call me again because my husband wouldn't like it. And when the Florida prosecutors wanted to meet with me, I could say it had to be at a time when my husband could be there.

I have been in and out of relationships since Hank, but with my trust and intimacy issues, it wasn't much fun. I tried to change and grow, but I decided that in the long run I would be happier as a single woman. I have many women friends, and those deep relationships mean the world to me. And I can't overstate the healing power of the animals in my life, especially my beloved cats, who bring much love and comfort to me every day.

As I rebuilt my life, I found that volunteering my time was helpful in addressing my feelings of failure because of my involvement with Ted Bundy. I held sick babies at a local hospital, did cat care for a rescue group, worked for the environment, helped seniors go grocery shopping and to appointments, and so on.

The number one thing that has allowed me to find peace after the catastrophe of Ted Bundy is my spiritual life. The church I grew up in forbade drinking alcohol, and I carried a lot of guilt during my periodic spurts of attendance as an adult. Once I quit drinking, I tried going again to see whether it was now a better fit. It wasn't. I then found a church that did feed my spiritual side and it dovetailed nicely with my recovery program. Between the two, I learned much about living life on life's terms.

As you'd know from reading *The Phantom Prince*, sound thinking was not my strong suit. The tools I've gained in my recovery have given me a new way of thinking and viewing life each day. And I've finally learned that no amount of intense, repetitive thinking is ever going to change the past. I've learned what "let it go" means.

I don't have an earthly explanation for what occurred starting that day in July 1974, when my coworker handed me the newspaper composite of the man suspected of a string of abductions. Earlier that day, I had read a different newspaper with a different composite sketch. I studied it closely, but it didn't look like anyone I knew. When I looked at the drawing handed to me, I saw that it did look *slightly* like my Ted. I immediately felt as if an unbearable weight had fallen on me.

My mind started racing. It felt crazy to even contemplate that the drawing looked like Ted. I tried to dismiss my concerns, *but I couldn't*. The more information that was revealed about the suspect, *the more I worried*. I was sure my fears were irrational, but still, *I couldn't stay silent*. Then, when police told me he wasn't their man, I tried to accept it, *but I couldn't*. I knew my fears about Ted had to be wrong, because I knew him so well. There was no way I would ever contact the police again, *but I did*. Given my fear and confusion, I was not strong enough to act on my own. Trying to apply logic to something that made no sense left me feeling helpless. I learned from this that grace isn't always pretty or ethereal, but grace is always working in my life when I get out of the way. I am grateful for the power of prayer, which gave me strength and guided me to do the right thing.

Most important: I love my daughter, Molly. I have deep regrets about the impact that my decisions have made on her life. Being a better mom is my priority, but I make mistakes all the time. Thankfully, she knows how much she is loved. Ted Bundy has been a part of her life since she was a little girl of three years old. She has faced her own challenges and has blossomed into a remarkable woman.

— MOLLY'S STORY —

Molly Kendall

As I set out to create a picture of my life with Ted for you, I have a big problem: I can't remember how it felt to love him. I had loved Ted with my entire heart, but when forced to accept the truth about who he really was, I could no longer sustain that love. I cannot love a person who enjoys torturing, raping, maiming, and killing women. As I gained the knowledge of who Ted was, I lost my faith in human beings, as well as my belief in God.

By creating my own story, one that makes sense to me, I have regained my faith. By surrounding myself with good people, I have found that I can trust the majority of the human race. As far as Ted is concerned, I can recall the things that we did together, but not the feelings of love that went along with them. That becomes a challenge as I invite you to step into my experience.

Yesterday I met with my mom to go through some of the many pictures that we have, hoping they would jog my memory of the feelings. My mom is the opposite of me. She has a hard time forgetting the feelings of love she and Ted shared. Along with the pictures, she also produced a huge box of letters Ted had written her.

As I looked at these letters, I saw more than a thousand hours' worth of his thoughts written there, pouring out his love for her. His hopes for her. His insights related to anything that he felt might draw her to him. I realized: She's not imagining this love. They had it. It was true for them. And it had been true for me, too. I left upset that I could not stick my experience back into a box with a tidy label on it: Psychopath, Sociopath, Lies, Ted's Alibi. All preferred over the label Love.

My mom and I are damn lucky to have lived through the experience of knowing Ted. Neither one of us has had to mourn the loss of the other. I have spent the bulk of my life grieving the loss of Ted's victims. I have been sickened and depressed by what happened to them at the hands of someone who chose to make me a pet instead of another victim.

Those whose lives were brutally taken away have been a constant presence for me. People have suggested that I have survivor's guilt. I reject that. We all should be alive. What I have is profound sadness and anger that some worthless dirtbag can come along and take away a family's bright and shining light, leaving a gaping hole that is never to be filled.

And I loved that worthless dirtbag. I thought of *him* as bright and shining. He was so smart. Looking at those letters yesterday, I saw that he was using words I still haven't learned. I forgot how smart he was. I forgot everything good about him. He had so much going for him, and at the core of it all was this hidden, evil, subhuman being. For the sake of this writing I will try to remember my feelings, but it all looks so different now.

I see why people are obsessed with figuring him out. For years, I thought continually about how this same person I loved could do these cruel and violent things. Finally, I was able to let go. I took on this mantra: He's crazy, and being sane, you will never understand crazy. Just give up. Live your life. You still have it. It's a gift.

MY HERO

The three-year-old me had loved Ted instantly. He delighted me by mixing up the words to my favorite story to make me burst out laughing at his ridiculous "mistakes." He knew just how to act to win me over. He was handsome, he dressed well. He made a heck of a first impression on my mother and me.

Ted quickly became a fixture in our lives. Deeming our shabby downtown apartment unsuitable, he helped us find a duplex in the Green Lake neighborhood of Seattle. That was fine with me. In the downtown place, the lady upstairs who watched me during the day had called me a brat for not letting her little boy play with my toys. I can see why she thought that. I piled them all under a blanket and sat on top of it, chasing her son away if he came near. I was afraid he would steal them, and then I would lose the only things that remained of my life in Utah. One night, as she and her family ate their dinner and stared at me sitting mournfully on my blanket mound, she told me that my mom had forgotten to pick me up and would probably never come for me.

The move to Seattle had been hard on me. Being the firstborn grandchild in both my mom's and my dad's families, I was very loved and celebrated by grandparents and aunts and uncles alike. We left them all behind, along with a rich family history and a sense of context. In Seattle it was just my mom and me. Strange places filled only with strangers. Constant raindrops on the windshield of our freezing-cold Volkswagen bug, the annoying whine of the windshield wipers a nauseating backdrop for my sad and lonely feelings.

When Ted came into our lives, suddenly we were golden. We had someone amazing to live life with. Ted knew Seattle, where to go, what to do for fun. He was there to hold my hand and play my new favorite game, "swing me," with my mom holding my other hand as we walked. He was so quick-witted and funny. He was physically expressive with his body and might break out in a dance or run and leap when playing with me. To make me laugh, he would sing in falsetto to the songs on the radio or mimic the cartoon voices of my favorite characters.

His manner was more polished than ours. He knew all the right things to say to any type of person to make a friend. His clothes and possessions, while not numerous, were cooler than ours. He liked our VW bug, though. So well that he ended up buying one for himself. Ours was that funny light blue color; his was tan with a sunroof that he would let my friends and me stick our heads out of while he drove. Ted brought so much joy into our lives. We felt really lucky that he was our guy.

What was it about my mom that made her different to Ted that night they met at a bar in the University District? Why did he not kill her? She was a naive, shy, sweet young woman of twenty-four. She was then, and is now, extremely lovable, but all Ted's victims were also lovable young women, each with her own list of good qualities.

Did Ted have a normal side to him that was simply a lonely guy looking for a girlfriend? My mom had approached him, saying he looked as if he had lost his best friend. She told him about our move from Ogden and how hard she was working to create a good life for me. Maybe, at that moment, these things put her in a different category for him.

Is it possible Ted could have been looking for a standing alibi to make himself appear more normal? I don't know. If he was, he sure got more than he bargained for. He eagerly stepped into the role of boyfriend, father figure, protector, and guide for our new life in Seattle.

As a young child, I thought Ted had some funny ideas. He preferred that I wear dresses instead of pants. He asked my mom to make the more conservative choice if asked to weigh in on her style. He thought I should be more respectful to my mom. Basically, he was old-fashioned in his preferences for us.

One night, shortly after Ted entered our lives, we were driving to Herfy's to eat hamburgers. I was being sassy to my mother. Ted outlined his plan to cure me of my brattiness: He told her that if I was being mouthy, then they must completely not acknowledge me. All talking to me would stop and they would speak of me to each other only as "the child." As in, "If the child apologizes and stops behaving that way, then we will speak to her again."

I had already lost almost every person in my life to this move. Now I only had my mom and Ted, and when they didn't speak to me, I was awash in loneliness. After the first application of this lesson I quickly learned to be a bit more well behaved. I remember this incident well, even though it made no impression at all on my mom. The scary thing about it was that this new guy was attempting to take charge of me, and I was afraid she just might let him.

We did all kinds of fun things together. Ted was always surprising me. During a visit to Seattle Center, Ted delighted me by leaping onto the carousel once it was in motion, unexpectedly appearing at my side. He was always doing things like that. Through my eyes, he was magical. He broke the rules in little ways that I adored. You could expect the unexpected.

In fact, Ted could run faster and jump higher than anyone I'd ever seen. My mom loved it when he would jump straight up and click his heels together in the air. She is not a very good photographer, though, and we have many pictures of his body doing this maneuver with his head cut off at the top of the frame. He was kind of like an animal in how connected he was to his body. Thought and action did not have the same separation that they seem to have for other humans.

Once, when we were at a friend's house, Ted was seated with his back to a window that had a radio balanced on its ledge. His chair must have been on its cord somehow, because when he rocked back it pulled the radio off the ledge and sent it careening toward the ground. Without moving his body, even to turn his head, he stuck his hand out behind him and caught it in the air. Just like that. It was like he had eyes in the back of his head.

Another time, my mom and Ted and I were at Northgate Mall. It was not an enclosed mall at that time, and we were walking along outside. Unexpectedly Ted took off running. A man across the parking lot had run past a woman, grabbed her purse, and taken off. She didn't scream; there was no commotion. My mom and I were oblivious, but Ted had seen the whole thing. He ran after the man and apprehended him, holding him until the police came. He received a commendation from the Seattle Police Department.

You know why he saw it? Because he was watching. He must have been watching her. Like a predator watches prey. Why did he intervene and act the hero this time? Even after all these years, I couldn't tell you.

We loved to visit Woodland Park Zoo. The reptile house was my favorite. Ted would hold me over the crocodile pit railing and make little moves like he was going to toss me in, saying, "I'm gonna drop you, I'm gonna drop you." I thought it was a fun game and would shriek and cling to him.

When I was five, my cat Loretta was pregnant. For some odd reason I had wanted to name her Honky Mustard, but lucky for her, I was overruled. She was white (and Honky is a derogatory term for a white person, in case you don't speak 1970s lingo), but I have no idea why I thought that was a good name. In any case, I knew that she was going to have kittens, but I had no idea what that actually meant.

One morning she started yowling in this strange way I hadn't heard before. She went behind the couch and started pooping out these pink blobs. "Mom! Mom! Get up! The cat is sick!"

My mom and Ted were sleeping in her room. They came out and told me that these were kittens. They were in sacks that Loretta was supposed to clean off them. One by one they became a bit more kitten-like, except this one that lay there real still. It was dead. My mom and I were heartbroken. Ted snapped into action, cleaning the tiny kitten and massaging its chest. We thought he had lost his mind. After a couple of minutes of this treatment, the kitten sprang to life. Ted made it live. My hero!

Our house was near Green Lake, and we loved to go there and float in our inner tubes. Ted once suggested we should go in after it was already dark. That was scary! He would swim down under the water and startle you by grabbing at you.

One summer day at Green Lake, Ted had brought his yellow inflatable raft. He and I took it out into the lake, and I was swimming around it for quite a while after having jumped out.

Exhausted, I went to get back in and as my hand touched the edge of the raft, Ted made two small strokes with the oars, sending the raft backwards a couple of feet. All the while watching my eyes with his own dead, hate-filled eyes. This was the first time I ever saw those eyes. The raft slipped from my fingertips.

I swam to the edge of it to try again. Same thing: He pulled the raft just out of reach, watching me begin to struggle. Back in those days, children weren't protected from every possible harm like they are now. I was not in a life jacket and was tired from my swim.

We repeated this scenario two more times. Floundering, I gave up and turned to swim the longer distance to the shore. Fortunately, I had had swim lessons in the summers. I made it to the shore exhausted, panting and crying. I collapsed onto the blanket where my mom was tanning herself. I told her what had happened. I knew he had done it to me on purpose.

My mom yelled at Ted when he rowed back to shore. "Liz, I thought she was a stronger swimmer than that. It was supposed to be a joke." She accepted this as the truth. So did I. I had been wrong in my perception. Why would Ted try to hurt me? He loved me.

Over the years, there were other variations on this theme of Ted "innocently" hurting me. A sudden body check sending me sprawling to the pavement, a football drilled full force into my face. Each time, I felt he had done it on purpose, but I chose to believe his explanations of why I was wrong.

I had never heard of gaslighting until the past decade of my life. There was a lot of that going on with Ted. You were always wrong if you thought Mr. Perfect could have had any ill intent whatsoever. You ended up feeling bad for questioning the integrity of such a marvelous person.

In 1972, we relocated from Green Lake to the University District. We were moving in, and several kids my age were playing outside on the street. I was terribly shy. Ted was not. "Hey, you kids, this is Molly, she's going to live here. What are your names? Want a Popsicle?" He worked his magic on them—easy joking and engaging conversation—and just like that, I had friends. I was on my way to being established in my new neighborhood.

YOU'RE "IT"

Our place in the U District was a giant old house that had once been grand. It had been split up into a few different apartments, and the upstairs was shared housing with a common kitchen and bathroom used by university students. Our apartment was in the middle of the house, which had once been the kitchen, dining room, and parlor. Shabby chic, 1970s style. At the back of the apartment was a tiny half bath with a separate shower located around the corner. I was "It." I stood up against the wall, hiding my eyes and counting to thirty.

Rushing out into the living room, I was surprised to find all the lights out. *Spooky!* I thought excitedly. I was now seven, and Ted had been appointed my babysitter for the night. It was unusual because if my mom was out, it was usually with him.

I saw him right away, even in the dark. He was curled up in the fetal position on the floor, a blue afghan that Granny had knitted for us covering him from head to toe. Worst hiding job ever! I started to pull the blanket off him and saw that he was completely undressed. "You're naked!" I accused, frowning.

"I know, but that's because I can turn invisible, but my clothes can't, and I didn't want you to see me!" And with that, he was off running, back to the home base that you touch so that you don't have to be "It."

I was confused. That made no sense at all, even though it sounded whimsical and cute. But I didn't want to be "It," so I stopped thinking and started running. Running to the back of the house to touch home base before him. We were laughing as we arrived at home base. It was right by the shower; I tried to shove him out of the way, and comedically, Ted fell down to the shower mat where he sat cross-legged, covering his penis with his two hands. Still cracking up, I wrestled with him, trying to pull his hands away. I succeeded, and I saw that he had an erection.

Being an only child, a girl, who lived with her mom, I'm not sure if I had ever seen a penis before, let alone an erection. It was kind of reddish purple and to my child eyes it looked like when you hit your thumb with a hammer or something, so I said, "Does it hurt?" He stopped laughing and looked up at me.

Something was very wrong. The pupils of his eyes had become tiny, almost as small as the point of a pencil. One was looking a slightly different direction from the other. "No, it doesn't hurt. . . ."

I wasn't really hearing him, I was searching for the person who I knew. That person was receding, farther and farther back, away from the eyes. It's as if the person who I loved was now at the end of a long hallway and we could barely see each other. And then he wasn't there anymore. But I saw something new seeing me. Something dangerous with those reptilelike eyes.

My mom had been making me go to the Mormon church. I

think because I was unruly, but she denies this. We came from Utah, descendants of Mormon pioneers. However, it was the 1970s in the University District, and culturally everything was very bohemian and free. But not at the church. There it was like the 1950s in Iowa, a whole other thing. But I made peace with it and took in the lessons they taught me. I was told that if I was in trouble, or wrestling with what to do, the Holy Ghost might talk to me. They said the Holy Ghost was the part of God that quietly speaks to you and helps guide you to make the right choices.

At that moment, having seen a physical change manifest in the naked man who was no longer my trusted friend Ted, I started to hear something. Maybe "hear" is the wrong word; it was like an invisible typist was typing inside of my head and the words came out as knowing. Somewhere deep inside my brain this quiet presence was feeding me instructions on how to remain safe: *Laugh and smile. Act as if nothing is wrong. Tell him you love him. Tell him this game has been really fun but that you are tired, and you would like to go to bed now.*

I see now how transparent I must have been. A child tap-dancing pitifully to get away from circumstances that were rapidly changing her world for the worse. But somehow it worked, and he agreed. We moved toward the bedroom.

Suddenly, he said, "Hey, I know . . . would you like me to get in bed with you and read you some Uncle Wiggily stories?" These are the books of Ted's childhood and he has been reading them to me. Uncle Wiggily is a rabbit who wears a suit of clothes, complete with top hat.

"No thanks," I said. "I'm tired." My escape plan is crumbling.

My memory of what happened next is fragmented. Ted challenges me. I am not going to be able to get away.

I get into the bed, which happens to be a top bunk, which is prone to collapsing. Ted was very agile and easily hops up there and lies behind me to read the book to me.

"You peed!" I blurt out, dismay and surprise overriding fear. The sheet was all wet. I don't remember what he said to explain this. I do know I tried to keep on acting like nothing was wrong. Loving, in fact, as the voice had instructed me to act.

My next memory is of him leaving my room. I lay awake in fear for a very long time, watching the door. Hoping he would not come back. He did not.

I never said one word to my mother about this until many years later. We loved Ted. He had been such a positive figure in our lives, such a help to her. I did not want him to get in trouble. I knew it wasn't right that he had been naked. I did not, at this point, understand the concept of sexual arousal. It was long after this that I figured out that penises were not always erections. Still, I did not want him to have to go away. I kept Ted's weird behavior to myself.

He stayed away for more days than was typical, and I thought that maybe he would never come back. Finally, he did, and there was some awkwardness between us at first that soon turned into more or less the usual dynamic that we had. Except that I no longer trusted Ted to act correctly toward me.

I began to guard myself more physically, trying to control his hands, which were on me too much for my comfort. Ted had always been very physical with me. Carrying me, swinging me, unmercifully tickling me. But now it was a much different experience.

In the pictures printed in this book from Christmas 1974, I am smiling but I remember feeling very uncomfortable and confused about how to behave. We are on a visit to my grandparents' house in Ogden. The night before this, Ted had grabbed a camera and run into the bathroom where I was naked in the tub. He took a picture of me, cringing and embarrassed. He told my grandmother, who was an avid photographer, "She will appreciate having this picture later!"

In the past, there had been other incidents that had troubled me. One was how he would carry me: he would put me in kind of a crotch hold. I remember that a couple of times his fingers had slipped inside my underwear and touched me.

This isn't right, my mind told me, but I was confused. Maybe it was accidental or maybe grown-ups just didn't care about what areas they touch you on. Maybe I was supposed to just accept it as normal, even if it made me feel gross.

One night at dinner, Ted scooped me onto his lap and did the crotch hold in front of my mom. "Ted!" she roared. "Do not hold her like that!"

"Oh, I didn't mean anything by it, Liz, geez. You are completely overreacting!" And then it was over, and he didn't do that anymore. There were always rational explanations, all of them involving the fact that we were misinterpreting or overreacting. By this time, I had been conditioned not to trust my own feelings. I pushed these incidents far beneath the sea of good times and memories that vastly outnumbered them. I loved Ted, and I wanted everything to be all right again.

THE TRUTH SINKS IN

It had been all over the local news that two women had been abducted from Lake Sammamish State Park near Seattle. Although my mother was tortured by her suspicions about Ted, she had not discussed them with me. I had teased Ted when the profile of the suspect came out. "Your name is Ted, his name is Ted, you drive a Volkswagen bug and so does the suspect! You know it's you!" He laughed it off. "Yes, that's right, Monkey, it's me. Ha-ha, real funny."

It wasn't funny now that Ted had been arrested. The situation had changed shape rapidly, in ways that confused me. Ted was charged with erratic driving and possession of burglary tools, then attempted abduction, and finally he became the chief suspect in multiple murders and disappearances. Shockingly, my mother had finally told me that she believed he might be guilty of these things.

I continued to love Ted and believe in his innocence with a child's unwavering steadfastness. I believed that in the end he would be exonerated of all wrongdoing. I awoke every day, suffocating in grief, as it sunk in that this was not a bad dream, this was happening, worsening. Day after day, the television talked about it, the papers talked about it, my friends' parents talked about it.

One day I gathered all the girls in my fifth grade class who I considered to be my friends. Some of them thought Ted was my father because over the years they had seen him do all those things a dad would do. I told them that I knew they might have heard these accusations against Ted, but I knew he was innocent and would be cleared. If they had any questions, they should come to me and ask me.

I believed with my whole heart that Ted was innocent. I wanted to tell everyone in the entire world that they were wrong, wrong, wrong. Even after he was convicted of attempted kidnapping, I thought it must be a case of mistaken identity. I could not believe the man who made my cocoa and taught me to ride a bike could do anything like this.

Ted had given my mom a copy of *Papillon*. A story of a wrongly accused man who escaped many times from multiple prisons. I was reading well above my grade level, and I devoured this book. It spoke to my belief in Ted's innocence. While awaiting trial for the murder of a woman in Colorado, Ted made his own daring escape, leaping from the second-story Colorado courthouse window. If people were talking about him before, suddenly it reached epic proportions. He was now a folk hero with a media frenzy of clever jokes and banter, even novelty T-shirts. I still wanted to scream it from the rooftops, how it was all a mistake.

He was recaptured within a week. But seven months later, Ted escaped a second time. This time I felt afraid. I had now realized that he knew my mother had gone to the police with her suspicions about him. For the first time I allowed myself to wonder, *What if he did these things? What if he comes here and tries to kill us?*

Instead he fled to Florida, where, we would later learn, he raped and murdered two sorority sisters at the Chi Omega house. He attacked three other women who did not die. He raped and killed and mutilated a girl of twelve, like me, Kimberly Leach.

When Ted was captured in Florida, the truth permeated my stubborn heart, that this was who he was, a murderer. I knew he called my mother the night he was recaptured, and, as she said, he "confessed without confessing." But it took a very long time for it to fully sink in, that this man I loved was a deranged monster who took great pleasure in hurting and killing women.

It was during the trial for the Chi Omega murders that I forced myself to assimilate the undeniable evidence presented. My mother had remained in Seattle, while I was with my grandparents for the summer as usual, only nothing was normal. Every day the first nationally televised murder trial played out before my eyes.

I don't think my grandparents understood what I was watching as I sat there day after day. As pictures of bloody gore that had been beautiful, vibrant young women, people's children, were displayed. As deep bite marks that fit the crooked, nightmarish teeth of Mr. Theodore R. Bundy were analyzed.

I learned all kinds of things during this trial. About types of sperm, forcible rape with objects, smashing of heads and garroting of necks.

Later, during the penalty phase of the Kimberly Leach trial, I learned that Ted now "loved" Carole Boone, as he proposed to her after putting her on the witness stand while acting as his own attorney. Remorseless doesn't begin to cover the circus-like way Ted used the televised proceedings to stroke his own ego at this trial for the rape, murder, and mutilation of a child.

This killing of the girl who was my own age has haunted me for many years. It is only recently that I have been able to stop the brutal details of her death from regularly playing out like a horror film before my eyes. I have grieved for her and her loved ones continually. In fact, for the majority of my life I have grieved over all the women who Ted murdered and attacked.

THE LAST LETTER

In the late 1980s, my mom went through an accelerated period of spiritual growth. She took classes, read books, prayed, and meditated. Ted was going to be executed. I think, in part, she was preparing herself for this.

I was living at home and had begun earning my associate's degree at North Seattle Community College. For the first time since Ted was arrested, I was doing well. I was on the dean's list. At this late date, I had finally learned what it meant to "apply yourself" to the process of learning. I went around meeting with my professors, explaining what was happening in my life. That I might have difficulty focusing, or might cry in class, but that I would be doing my best to keep on with my good work. I'd be damned if I would let Ted screw me up again.

Over the past years the guy had continually resurfaced. Running his mouth. Manipulative lies, all of it. Nothing he ever said was the truth. I was filled with a deep, cold hatred as I watched him. Evil asshole. I was looking forward to death silencing him for good.

One day when I arrived home from school, a letter had come in the mail. It had the prison address on it. My mom was still at work. Although it was addressed to my mother, I opened it. Somehow, over thousands of miles, Ted had been able to seize on just the right things to say to hook my mom into his toxic drama again. He talked about how he found God and was working on his spiritual program. I can't remember what else he professed. The reason I can't remember? I

207

burned that letter in the fireplace, right then and there, and never said one word about its arrival.

It was all the things my mom would have wanted to hear. I was unwilling to watch her be ripped to shreds again by this "love." Fuck that. Leave us alone. Leave the whole country alone. Nobody, save your mother, cares that you say you found God, as you try to bargain with the remains of the women you tortured and killed, to save your sorry life. Time to die.

I remember nothing of the day of the execution.

The next thing that I remember happening is that Ted's civil rights attorney from death row contacted my mother. Apparently, one of his last wishes was for us to be told that he really had loved us. Because, as she put it, "he knew you would wonder, given the circumstances. Also, Liz, he wondered why you did not respond to his letter."

I had to confess to my mother that I burned it. She understood the reasons I gave as to why I did it. She accepted my reasons in a quiet fashion. It was her mournful manner that made me see that if you turned the situation another way, I had robbed her of some closure.

As for robbing Ted of his precious Liz? Not sorry. Not one bit sorry. I honestly would have taken him out back and shot him myself rather than let him hurt one more person.

COURAGE

For many years I tried to drown my grief in alcohol, drugs, smoking, and reckless behavior of all kinds. As anyone who is a recovering addict can tell you, that didn't work. It only gave me more things to be remorseful over. I finally was able to become sober when I decided to turn around and face what I was running from. As of this writing, I have thirteen years of sobriety.

Another action I took to move forward was to attempt to join a local support group for the families and friends of victims of violent crimes. I say attempt, because when I told them what my link to violent crime was, they let me know that it would be potentially upsetting to the other members of the group for me to join, since they were connected to Ted's crimes through his victims.

After the understanding of that sunk in, I asked if they would please ask around and see whether any of these group members would be willing to exchange a letter with me. They found someone: A mother of one of the victims was willing to receive my letter. I told her about my anguish over her loss of her daughter and how much I thought about these young women every day of my life. She wrote me the most healing reply.

I was shocked when I read her words, that over the years she had wondered how my mother and I were doing. I'd feared that she hated us; far from it, she had hoped we were able to heal. She said that undeniably, it was beyond shattering for her to go through the experience of losing her daughter to murder, but that as the years passed, she was choosing to bravely move forward and be happy once more.

Her refusal to let Ted Bundy take the rest of her life from her inspired me. What a remarkable, strong person. I wanted to be like her and do the same.

I decided to begin by reclaiming Lake Sammamish State Park as a place of peace and freedom for me and my dogs to walk. I was so frightened of it, even by the name. I went to great lengths never to go anywhere near the place.

It was terrifying to visit there the first time. With my heart in my throat, I practically ran down one of the trails, stiffly dragging my dogs along. Fearing what was behind each bend in the path, I felt my heart hammer in my chest.

I have spent countless hours there now. Most often in the rain. Without a human companion, but with my beloved dogs, I have walked everywhere a person can go in those 512 acres, no matter how remote. There is no path that I have not walked down, and I have seen some amazing things:

A large stag with a full rack, kneeling to rest in the tall grass.

A coyote who seemed to be dancing and leaping beneath a tree. Who, upon catching sight of me and my dogs, did an up-close, run-by viewing, all the while looking as if he was grinning at us.

A juvenile eagle who, with a fierce cry, flew at eye level between me and a strange man who was making me nervous, making the man jump back and hurry away. Maybe the eagle was saying thanks for my solitary version of a Native American fancy dance, done to pay tribute the first time I saw him in the sky over the field.

And best of all, two adult eagles who, after singing all day in the rainy woods, grabbed each other's feet and did a barrel roll out of the sky right toward my head, parting at the last second and flying away.

And now I am moving forward by allowing myself a voice. For years I have quietly listened as others have told parts of my story. I stayed quiet out of fear. Fear of exposing myself publicly. And because I wanted to live a life of my own creation, not one that endlessly orbits this evil man's story. But most of all, I remained quiet out of fear that my perspective would further hurt the others—the victims' loved ones and Ted's family—who, like me, have been repeatedly hurt by the continual reemergence of this story.

I have come to realize that I am not protecting anyone by silencing myself. By doing that, I only throw away my ability to live life fully. It is healing to share my perspective. I look forward to hearing the experiences of the other people impacted by Ted Bundy when the time feels right to them. The bravery and perspective of those who have told their stories already have been an inspiration.

And now I go forward, with my new mantra: Life is a gift and you still have it. Have the courage to be happy.